COMMON
SENSE

THOMAS PAINE

COMMON SENSE

FALL RIVER PRESS

New York

FALL RIVER PRESS

New York

An Imprint of Sterling Publishing
387 Park Avenue South
New York, NY 10016

FALL RIVER PRESS and the distinctive Fall River Press
logo are registered trademarks of Barnes & Noble, Inc.

This 2013 edition published by Fall River Press.

Cover design: Jason Chow
Cover illustration: Paul Girard

ISBN: 978-1-4351-4601-3

Printed and bound in China

10 12 14 16 18 20 19 17 15 13 11

www.sterlingpublishing.com

Contents

NOTE ON THE TEXT

In the original text of *Common Sense,* Thomas Paine mixed British and American spellings of certain words, as well as archaic and standard spellings. For this edition, the publisher has adopted standard American usage in the few instances where this was inconsistent in Paine's original text. Paine's style of punctuation and noncapitalization of some proper nouns has been retained.

Introduction

I. "A Life Lived to Some Purpose"

1

BYSTANDERS PASSED EN ROUTE WOULD HARDLY have noticed, the scene was so ordinary. Barely more than a dozen mourners joined the procession journeying from Greenwich Village to New Rochelle, on June 9, 1809, to bury Thomas Paine and honor his memory. Paine, English by birth, died at seventy-two unheralded and quite nearly forgotten in his adopted land—a peculiar and poignant fate for a man who had been his century's most notorious revolutionary.

On the grounds of Paine's modest farm, a gift from the state of New York in gratitude for his services during the American Revolution, the small group gathered around the gravesite. There stood Mme. Bonneville who tended Paine during his last illness, her two sons, a few friends, a group of Irishmen attending to honor Paine's opposition to English domination of their homeland, and two free blacks wishing to pay their respects to one who had been among the first to editorialize against slavery.

As the mahogany coffin was lowered into the ground, Mme. Bonneville instructed her son Benjamin to stand with her by Paine's grave while she offered the simple benediction: "Oh! Mr. Paine! My son stands here as testimony of the gratitude of America, and I, for France." Paine, the intellectual firebrand at the center of disquiet and revolution in England, America, and France, once provided a friend his own testimonial, writing that having a hand in two historic revolutions was to enjoy a "life lived to some purpose."

2

THE ORIGINS OF GENIUS ARE ALWAYS SOMETHING of a mystery, but in Paine's case this is especially true, for of his first four decades we have little evidence with which to reconstruct the essential facts of his life. The picaresque and romantic turns of Paine's public career, however, would suit the hero of a Fielding novel. Born in 1737, Paine rose above poverty, obscurity, and failure only when, nearly forty and after abandoning England to emigrate to the American colonies, he achieved a stunning success with the publication of his pamphlet *Common Sense*. As a pamphleteer, only Karl Marx's influence has outstripped Paine's.

Once Paine had settled in Philadelphia, with a letter of introduction from Benjamin Franklin (whom Paine had met through acquaintances in England) to assist him, success and fame came quickly. He obtained employment as editor of the *Pennsylvania Magazine,* which provided Paine the opportunity to write and publish his own work. During the brief time he was associated with the journal, Paine managed to print a series of short essays that gave evidence of an uncommonly independent and adventurous mind. It is remarkable and curious, too, that Paine could so quickly display the power of so accomplished a writer, for where he previously had found the opportunities to hone his skills is largely unknown. But in short order Paine produced editorials arguing for more lenient divorce laws, humane treatment for animals, an end to dueling, justice for women, and the eradication of slavery. Paine's opposition to slavery, a cause he supported throughout his public life, resulted within weeks in the creation of the first American Anti-Slavery Society.

The writing and publication of *Common Sense* followed, and with it fame. Paine was soon known throughout the American colonies and across Europe. The political tract immediately became the moral and intellectual touchstone for American colonists struggling to articulate their case for independence from England. It received an enormous hearing abroad as well, although sometimes in truncated editions: the French, who delighted in Paine's savage lampooning of British institutions and imperial power, censored those passages that argued the case against monarchy.

With the colonies committed to revolution, Paine took up arms as a private in General Washington's army and later served as an aide-de-camp to General Greene. During the bleakest moments of the war when the Americans were tottering near defeat, he began issuing a series of essays (*The Crisis* papers), written by firelight late at night, that when read to the assembled troops hardened the resolve of the dispirited men. "These are the times that try men's souls," Paine wrote. "The summer soldier and the sunshine patriot will, in this crisis, shrink from the service of his country; but he that stands it now, deserves the thanks of man and woman." Paine served for a period as the Secretary to the Congress's Committee on Foreign Affairs, even visiting France in a mission to procure aid for the colonies. Afterward, serving as the Clerk to the Pennsylvania Assembly, he helped shape and gain passage for Pennsylvania's new constitution, a document at that time striking for its radically democratic sentiments.

3

AFTER THE WAR FOR INDEPENDENCE WAS WON, Paine eventually decided to return to Europe, and in 1787 he made the crossing first to France and shortly afterward to England. Although he had always harbored the hope that the spirit of revolution he had helped advance in America would arise in his homeland, his focus on returning home was not with politics but science. Paine, who all his life was fascinated by the natural sciences, and who possessed mathematical ability that under different circumstances might well have provided for a distinguished engineering career, set to work on designs for the first single-span iron bridge.

He did not ignore politics. Paine kept company among the intellectuals and political reformers (the poet William Blake and the philosopher William Godwin were two of the gifted in their number) who comprised the Revolution Society and the London Corresponding Society. Because of his fame, Paine was accorded a place of honor and leading role in discussions.

Events in France, however, cast a deep shadow over Europe and England. Paine traveled back and forth between England and France, preoccupied with hopes of obtaining endorsements from the leading scientific societies of the day—which his working prototype for an iron bridge eventually earned, although the windfall profits he imagined might follow never materialized. When in Paris the Bastille was overrun, Lafayette himself made a gift of the hated prison's key to Paine as a symbol of France's friendship and regard for America. But optimism about events in France was shaken when news of the Terror reached England; fear spread through every level of English society. When Edmund Burke addressed Parliament to warn of the dangers loosed in France, and then bitterly assailed the revolution's political ambitions and leaders in his *Reflections on the Revolution in France*, Paine was provoked to defend the revolution with his own *The Rights of Man*, which appeared in March 1791.

The book was a sensation. But the English authorities, frightened by disturbances in England and the events unfolding across the Channel, and fearing Paine's influence and past success in encouraging insurrection, brought charges of sedition against him. Sales of *The Rights of Man* were suppressed and booksellers were prosecuted. Paine himself, warned that he was being sought by the authorities, barely evaded capture before escaping England to France. In his absence he was convicted of high treason.

His reputation preceding him, Paine landed on the French coast at Calais to learn he was the city's elected deputy to the National Convention. That he could not speak or read French did not appear to greatly trouble the citizens of Calais, nor for that matter Paine. He proceeded a hero to Paris where, restricted in his social contacts by his English, he kept company mostly with the upper middle-class intellectuals associated with the politically moderate Girondin party. Addressing the Convention with the aid of a translator, Paine was the first—as he had been in America—to advocate abolishing the monarchy. And as he had experience of making a constitution, Paine was named to the committee charged with drafting a document for the assembled body's consideration. But before long, Paine's allies lost control of the Convention to the more radical Jacobin party, and political violence quickly escalated. Despite the dangers of the altered circumstances, Paine exhibited great personal bravery by urging the unsympathetic representatives to spare the King's life and impose a sentence of exile.

Although he held American citizenship, Paine was put at grave risk by the acceleration of the Terror. In the comparatively restrained political world of the American colonies, shaped by the same civil traditions that structured English life, Paine's voice had carried a radical provocation; but in France he was caught in depths of violent political struggle he did not understand and which threatened to drown him. He was in water well over his head, unable to read the currents with the instincts of one intimately familiar with the language, customs, and class animosities of the French. In Paris, unlike in the colonies, Paine's liberal opinions were overtaken rapidly by events and came to epitomize the cautious voice of conservative restraint amidst revolutionary turmoil.

He was committed to Luxembourg Prison where he languished, sick beyond hope of recovery, for ten months; only a jailer's oversight and Robespierre's timely fall from grace enabled Paine to elude the guillotine. When freed, he lived for a period with James Monroe, then serving as the American ambassador to France. Paine was even readmitted to the National Convention.

But Paine by then had been soured by the revolution's abandonment of its own high ideals, and to Monroe and his acquaintances Paine vented rage against those old friends (chiefly President Washington) whom he imagined had betrayed him, leaving him to rot in Luxembourg Prison.

In time Paine turned his attention elsewhere. He completed the last great literary labor of his life, *The Age of Reason,* a composition undertaken and its first part finished before his imprisonment, which provided a synopsis of the Enlightenment's deist beliefs. Paine would carry to his death the reputation of an atheist—wrongly, for he did not deny the existence of God, only the divinity of Jesus Christ. Although his views of religion were not so uncommon, for nearly all the most prominent American Founding Fathers were known to admit in private to beliefs resembling Paine's, the ardor with which he attacked Christian pieties and their supposed ground in the Bible was new and startling. His explicit expressions of disbelief roused the faithful to fury and earned Paine an enmity that destroyed the good reputation he enjoyed for his earlier activities in behalf of the American cause.

But to America, his adopted homeland, Paine eventually returned in 1802. He returned, however, to a country determined to ignore him: his polemics against President Washington had lost him the loyalty of many patriots, and his religious beliefs had earned him the wrath of the Christian faithful. His health, never firm after his imprisonment, was failing. He rarely could summon sufficient energy to address the issues of the day; social isolation only increased his misery. At the last, far along in illness and facing death, Paine turned to the Quakers and requested permission for burial in a Quaker graveyard. But his request was denied. Shortly afterward Paine died—defiant and unbowed to the end.

4

EVEN WHEN DEAD PAINE WAS NOT PERMITTED TO rest. In 1819, ten years after he had died, the English writer William Cobbett visited Paine's New Rochelle gravesite and dug up his bones. Absconding with the stolen skeleton, Cobbett embarked for England. While he lived, Cobbett had scorned Paine and even denounced him in print; but later Cobbett was convinced he had underestimated Paine and became his champion. Cobbett plotted to return Paine's bones to England where Paine might receive the honor due him.

The bones were lost, although just when and where has always remained a matter for conjecture. Some believed they were lost in a storm at sea, which would almost be fitting—Paine caught, in death as in life, drifting between the continents. But there is evidence that Cobbett displayed the bones upon arriving in England, and later they were reportedly offered at auction as part of the Cobbett estate, but the auctioneer refused to permit their sale. The bones perhaps were reburied in a garden plot belonging to Cobbett family heirs. Or most of them anyway, for reports surfaced every few decades of someone claiming to be in possession of Paine's skull, jawbone, or some other piece of his skeleton. Paine's final resting place (curiously, like his great foe Edmund Burke's) is a mystery.

II. THE PUBLICATION AND ARGUMENT
OF *COMMON SENSE*

1

Common Sense FIRST APPEARED ON JANUARY 10, 1776, and the exquisite stroke of luck it enjoyed upon its appearance could hardly have been calculated to greater effect. The pamphlet was published simultaneously with the arrival in Philadelphia of the text of King George III's recent speech to Parliament, which declared the American colonies were in open rebellion against the Crown. During the preceding year, Americans had engaged English troops in the first pitched battles of an increasingly militant independence movement. Massachusetts was the active center of resistance, for Boston served as headquarters to British troops in America; bloody fighting took place at Lexington, Concord, and especially at Breed's Hill, a site across

Boston Bay. And in September 1775, an American army moved north into Canada and laid siege to Quebec City. Those troops remained in Canada, occupying Montreal, at the time Paine was drafting *Common Sense.*

War, then, of some sort obviously was underway, but most colonists remained in deep conflict over the political ends being sought. Was this a war for independence? Certainly Sam Adams, John Adams, and Benjamin Franklin (who had just returned from England, where he had met and befriended Paine) hoped so; but theirs was still a minority opinion, both within the Continental Congress and among citizens at large. Most colonists probably held to a position defended by Franklin's fellow Philadelphian John Dickinson. He hoped for concessions from Parliament that would acknowledge the justice of colonial claims and address long-standing grievances—and maintain England and America's ties unbroken.

Advocates for outright independence from the British empire were rather few, and with good reason. For one, the colonies had little sense of themselves as possessing a shared identity to unite them against England. Colonial interests were far too many and divergent to suggest where ground for consensus might lie. England, moreover, was the world's most formidable power, and if the colonies were improbably to succeed in breaking free of her grip, they might face having to stave off challenges from England's European rivals. But perhaps most profoundly, the colonists knew their quarrel with England was a family quarrel: the liberties they sought were traditional English liberties. As family relations with England had been, on balance, sources for positive good, there was a fearful reluctance to sever union with the motherland.

These were the circumstances into which Paine's *Common Sense* made its intervention. Paine first thought to publish his essay in installments as letters to newspapers, but editors were reluctant to publish the work, either in part or whole. A friend of Paine's, Dr. Benjamin Rush, who both encouraged Paine to write the work and supplied him with its title, put the author in touch with Robert Bell, a printer with a reputation for bravery. It was agreed that Bell would keep half the profits, while Paine donated his share for the benefit of those American soldiers then engaged in Canada. Precautions were taken; the pamphlet appeared anonymously, its title page indicating only that the work was "By an Englishman."

Both men must surely have been flabbergasted by the public response to their undertaking—it was a publishing success without precedent. The pamphlet's first printing of several thousand copies sold out in days, and the second, with additions, sold just as quickly. Pirated editions soon circulated, and throughout the colonies newspapers carried substantial excerpts. Nineteen American and seven British editions made it to print. A hasty, abridged French translation followed. The best sales estimates range from Paine's own claim that 120,000 copies sold within three months of publication to a contemporary biographer's estimate that perhaps 500,000 copies sold within a year. The extent to which Paine's pamphlet reached literate citizens in the colonies—let alone readers abroad—can only be guessed at, but by any count it was extraordinarily high.

2

HISTORIAN ISAAC KRAMNICK NOTES THAT although the United States owes its existence in part to the incendiary brilliance of *Common Sense,* we must advance far into the essay before encountering its first substantial reference to America, and this should not surprise us. For Paine published the pamphlet only fourteen months after arriving in the colonies. He knew little of life here in America. Hardly a native, he was English through and through, and the bitter tones of his prose, in Kramnick's words, are an echo of "the theoretical mind and raging anger of English radicalism." The arguments of *Common Sense* divide into four principal sections, at least in its original edition, for subsequent printings produced a text a third as large, including a postscript and appendix with Paine's response to those Quakers who objected to his non-pacifist views.

Paine's first section is a history of mankind with themes (the state of nature and the social contract) drawn from the liberal English philosopher John Locke. Paine, following Locke's exposition of a century earlier, maintains that men once lived in a state of nature—solitary, isolated, and free—unconstrained by any form of government. He writes in a famous formulation that "society in every state is a blessing, but government even in its best state is but a necessary evil; in its worst state an intolerable one." For, Paine continues, "Government, like dress, is the badge of lost innocence; the palaces of kings are built on the ruins of the bowers of paradise." But men draw together for mutual protection and the satisfaction of common needs. And strangers who find themselves in a distant land (the colonists) will naturally unite and undertake the burden of self-government, and in doing so, shape for themselves republican institutions of government. Government is unavoidable for moral virtue does not govern the world, even if "the simple voice of nature and reason say it is right."

England's ruling institutions, celebrated internationally, are not truly republican; only the House of Commons, Paine says, can claim to be a republican form of government. But its rightful powers are checked by the "base remains of two ancient tyrannies," the person of the king and the landed aristocracy. The true will of the land, in England as in France, remains the king's. This leads Paine to another line of argument in the second section, which attacks the principle of monarchy and the soundness of hereditary succession.

The author inquires into the origins of monarchy. As Paine insists that all people are "equals in the order of creation," he wonders how it is possible that one family can establish itself in dominion over all others, for no natural or religious reasons for distinguishing one line from all others seem to justify such an arrangement. Paine readily resorts to scripture to show that the ancient Hebrews were condemned as sinful for desiring a monarchy, in imitation of heathen peoples, when they could be a free and republican people instead. And as heathens are the originators of monarchies, the authority of scripture cannot then be invoked in their favor.

Likewise, too, for the claims of superiority made in support of heredity succession. No one by reason of birth, Paine says, can possess the right to fix the standing of his own descendants favorably over all others. One ruler's electors cannot cede away the rights of posterity. England's troubles follow from its monarchy and heredity succession. If the lineages of kings are traced to their origins, one discovers "nothing better than the principal ruffian of some restless gang." Paine notoriously characterizes William the Conqueror as a "French bastard landing with an armed banditti and establishing himself king of England against the consent of the natives." And monarchies, Paine further contends, cause wars and civil conflicts, for they tempt the ambitious to conspire against the throne in its weakest moments—old age and infancy—while the people are made to suffer the consequences.

Common Sense's third section focuses directly on the American colonies. Here the clear, urgent objective is to cajole hesitant colonists into accepting that a break with England was both inevitable and justified. Relations with England had become so intolerable, Paine claimed, that only complete independence from the British empire would suffice; the time for debate was over and "arms as a last resource decide the contest." Independence would prove the key to insuring American security against corrupt European powers. A free America could rid itself of England's burdensome concern for military preeminence, devoting energies instead toward becoming a trading port to the world. America faced a unique opportunity to win genuine freedom: now it might become the haven for the world's wretched masses. The colonists must "receive the fugitive, and prepare in time an asylum for mankind."

After offering suggestions for the shape of a Continental government, Paine turns, anticlimactically, in the fourth section to a summary view of the colonies' strengths. He ventures the surprising judgment that in war with Britain, America would emerge the victor. Now the colonies must make their case to the world, he says, to inform everyone of their mistreatment at the hands of the English. It was time to prepare a manifesto, a declaration of independence, to obtain for America's cause vital recognition and support from foreign powers.

III. THE POWER OF PAINE'S STYLE

CLARITY, ESSAYIST E. B. WHITE SUGGESTED IN celebration of English plain style, is not the only virtue of good writing, but "since writing is communication, clarity can only be a virtue." It is the obvious and exemplary strength of Paine's prose. In an age noteworthy for the brilliance of its political writing, Paine was the eighteenth century's most gifted political journalist (that is, if that word is permitted to embrace the roles of public advocate and propagandist). *Common Sense* remains the most accomplished and stirring sample within the remarkably large and distinguished body of pamphlet literature inspired by the American Revolution.

Paine's ideas were not original. His intellectual debts are obvious and embody to an uncommonly pure degree the letter and spirit of Enlightenment liberalism. And while Paine possessed tireless intellectual curiosity, he was not a logically precise or exacting thinker. In *Common Sense*, it is possible to spot Paine reversing field shamelessly and incautiously against his earlier conclusions when he thinks it will advance the argument at hand. Friends said of Paine that he was a restless reader, impatient with books, and happiest when buried in newspapers or engaged in conversation driven by drink and a tavern's conviviality. But Paine had a knack for making the most of his limited education. In any case, strength of intellect—which indeed he possessed—was hardly the source of his influence as a pamphleteer.

Literary genius was. Paine owned the imagination and vigor of a consummate prose stylist. *Common Sense* is exceptional for its language, its striking phrases and clean clarity, its sentences as brilliant as glass. Two influences are at work here: the Quaker virtues of sincerity and direct address are joined to the Enlightenment belief in universal moral principles grounded in "common sense." The use of idiomatic language was a rhetorical effect that Paine, always an exacting craftsman, consciously exploited; but his lucidity is an achievement marking the advance (quite broadly in the eighteenth century) of a new aesthetic in rhetoric. T. S. Eliot said that the emergence of a new verse form always occasions a revolution in consciousness. Such moments, whether these involve a new verse scheme or a new aesthetic, profoundly implicate the forms of moral and political discourse.

The revolution in style that Paine's writing in key part initiated had the effect, too, of greatly widening the proper boundaries of public debate—almost an extension of the franchise itself. The style's luminous clarity and highly compressed power made *Common Sense*'s arguments accessible to nearly every colonial reader, empowering most colonists to engage in political debate on the daunting challenges they faced. Paine's impact bears comparison (if one allows for the disparity in significance) with the first translations of the Old and New Testaments into the languages of early modern Europe, occasions that furthered the democratic end of diffusing the tremendous power held by a few by allowing most to encounter and interpret the religious texts for themselves in their native tongues. Luther's astonishing literary and scholarly feat, translating the entire Bible into German, not only forged a new religious identity but helped shape a young language and nascent political identity as well.

Missing in *Common Sense* are the classical allusions and the tags of Greek and Latin quotation that were the rule for "elevated" composition in Paine's day. In their place Paine uses superbly evocative imagery borrowed from everyday life. Where contemporaries cited Virgil or Cicero, he draws upon a tradesman's experience or from science or medicine. Images of health and sickness, of youth and old age abound; these are concrete, vivid, often startling. They underscore the corruption and decrepit condition of Europe's monarchies beside America's youthful spirit and virtuous republican institutions. Paine's rhetorical verve rarely slackens; coupled with his extreme self-possession and nervy confidence in his own powers of judgment, these gifts remain the sources of his enduring power as a writer.

Contemporaries were at once dumbfounded by and intrigued with the pamphlet's "impudent" voice, for such candid expressions of contempt and dismissal were utterly new to public debate in the colonies—but hardly so in the debating circles that Paine had frequented in England, where he earned a reputation for the stubborn ferocity with which he defended his opinions. No colonist had risked expressing himself in print in so frankly rude and condescending terms toward the King. Americans were edging toward open rebellion, but with the expanse of the Atlantic to keep the full strength of England's dominating hand at bay, tensions fell short of the boiling point. Even in quarrel there was civility and respect for form. But Paine, who only recently had left the heat of England's kitchen, carried in his voice the wounded class rage of English radicalism. It was a voice to send temperatures soaring in the American colonies.

Paine's skill as a polemicist ultimately lay in the uncanny psychological insight he displayed in raising to consciousness the underlying assumptions of the American colonists. These assumptions, precisely because they were so widely shared, passed unmentioned, and in this way exercised an unconscious control on the public's imagination; exposing these to scrutiny, Paine broke their hold upon the public's will. After reading *Common Sense*, the colonists discovered they could now believe inevitable what only a short time earlier had seemed preposterous: breaking with the Crown and English rule.

IV. THOMAS PAINE'S LIBERALISM—AND OURS

1

PAINE WAS DRIVEN BY AN UNRELENTING HATRED for the existing social order. John Adams, who always regarded Paine warily and with disapproval, said he was a man to tear a house down, but who lacked the skills to rebuild it. The remark conveys the reservations about Paine's character and ability that many among his contemporaries held during his lifetime, and that have often informed the historical evaluations of his career. But Paine's achievements by any measure were exceptional: these were emblematic of the profound changes underway within the moral and political practices of the culture. He helped fashion a revolution in political rhetoric and moral discourse—"a trans-valuation of morals"—that ushered in a New World of liberal values displacing the Old World of aristocratic entitlement.

But if we are Paine's heirs, how should we honor Paine's legacy today? We might begin, first, by attending the difficulties of our characterizing that legacy. Put to one side Paine's scathing attacks upon monarchism in the name of republicanism and ask: Was Paine truly a republican? Historian Christopher Lasch claimed there is relatively little to tie him to the civic republican tradition. Lasch says Paine remained untroubled, for example, by the Anti-Federalist (republican) preoccupation with preserving for citizens the right of direct representation. He did not anticipate, either, what consequences would follow a division of political labor and the steady expansion of the nation's borders. With hindsight, it is possible to see that both developments have greatly eroded those civic republican virtues and loyalties that flourish only with face-to-face politics.

Certainly Paine, true to his own roots, always championed the small businessman (the tradesmen and shopkeepers); he did not envision the symbiotic growth of big business and big government that is so marked a feature of contemporary life. Paine's world was still largely agrarian. Ours is post-industrial and organized by the priorities of the multinational corporations. He claimed that monarchies are conspiracies propped in place by mystification and ignorance to exploit the people; taxation is systematic plunder exacted from citizens under threat of war. Nations, once freed of monarchies and devoted to commerce, would abolish war and foster universal citizenship. (A mordant phrase of Randolph Bourne's—"War is the health of the State"—sounds the hollowness of those claims.) The Anti-Federalists, however, were suspicious of commerce and disdained the cosmopolitan citizenship that Paine idealized. Citizenship, they believed, is rooted in the patriotic love of a particular place and people.

Was Paine a liberal then? Not if by liberalism we mean all that term has come to mean today, but his core beliefs were the premises of the

Enlightenment's philosophical liberalism—its moral and political and economic individualism. Paine's entire theory of government and society, summarized in *The Rights of Man,* elaborates a liberal theory of rights. When he speaks of duties, he does so only to underscore the guarantee to others of those same rights we would claim for ourselves. With regard to natural rights, Paine's interest lies entirely in distinguishing the state's obligation to realize the rights of its citizens.

2

WHAT ARE OUR POLITICAL ATTACHMENTS? Do these borrow from Paine's example? William Butler Yeats observed that things reveal themselves in the moment of their passing. Our polls confirm the suspicion daily: we are a people increasingly fearful of politics and uneasy with the claims of public life. But it was not always so. De Tocqueville, visiting the United States several decades after Paine's death, thought that to deprive an American of his politics would deprive him of half his life.

Expert opinion has in recent decades usually chosen to regard political passivity as evidence of the country's general health and maturity; certainly our political elites have long believed that the nonparticipation of significant minorities among the electorate ensures a desirable stability to political affairs. They prefer to say this under their breath, and they leave unsaid the truth that in liberal-democratic politics the costs of consensus are paid by those who are denied a voice in shaping it.

Part of American liberalism's crisis is that liberalism has distanced itself from its past in ways which contemporary liberals (and in the United States we are all liberals) fail to comprehend. Current debates over big government, affirmative action, activist judicial reform, university curricula, abortion, and "politically correct" norms of behavior are only seemingly isolated episodes: they are the sites of confrontation in the larger cultural war over the meaning of our American liberal tradition and our desires for the future. These debates extend disputes that have divided Americans since Paine's *Common Sense* first goaded the colonies toward nationhood. We attempt to honor at once the values of equality and freedom; but these values can only coexist in tension with one another. As many observers of American life have ironically noted, it can sometimes seem that our political parties conspired to divide the nation's moral capital between them.

Recent dissension within American liberalism reveals the influence of two formative visions still at work among us: an eighteenth-century republican vision of men and women bound together in community and virtue, and a nineteenth-century vision of free-market enterprise. Our civic republican ideal imagines that the laws that bind us together should be expressive of those moral goods we share as a people. Our free-market ideal, however, presumes that laws provide us the (neutral) constraints necessary for the unimpeded conduct of a civil society. If by our republican ideal moral goods are held in common, so that the moral goods of an individual are the community's moral goods as well, our free-market ideal contends that shared moral goods are (or are nearly) nonexistent. These opposed visions of public life are once again in open conflict.

—Gregory Tietjen
1995

CHRONOLOGY OF
THOMAS PAINE'S LIFE

1737 Born on January 29, in village of Thetford in Norfolk County, England. Parents are Joseph and Frances Cook Pain.

1750 Formal education ends at age 13. Becomes an apprentice to his father as a staymaker (corsets).

1753 Two attempts to run away to sea. The second is successful but short-lived. Serves almost a year at sea.

1757 Takes employment with a London shop as a staymaker. Eagerly attends city's public lectures on Newtonian science and philosophy.

1759 Opens his own shop and marries Mary Lambert, who dies after a year of marriage—possibly in childbirth.

1762 Fails at business and enters the customs service as an exciseman in Lincolnshire.

1765 Dismissed from service after attempting to organize the customs officers.

1771 Second marriage, to Elizabeth Ollive.

1772 Drafts pamphlet, *Case of the Officers of Excise,* his first known composition, which wins praise and some attention in Parliament.

1774 Loses post with the customs service. Obtains legal separation from his wife for reasons which neither party discloses. Emigrates to America and arrives on November 30, bearing a letter of introduction from Benjamin Franklin.

1775 Appointed editor of *Pennsylvania Magazine.* His essays begin to attract notice and influential friends in Philadelphia.

1776 Publishes *Common Sense.* Enlists in army, serving as an aide-de-camp to General Greene. Begins writing *The Crisis* essays.

1777 Obtains Congressional post as secretary to Committee on Foreign Affairs.

1779 Appointed clerk to Pennsylvania Assembly.

1781 Makes diplomatic mission to France for aid to the American cause.

1783 Writes last of *The Crisis* essays (#16).

1785 Works on various inventions, chiefly a design for a single-span iron bridge.

1787 Recrosses the Atlantic to France, pursuing approval for his bridge design.

1788 Returns to England to visit his mother. Meets Edmund Burke.

1790 Back in France. Given the key to the Bastille from Lafayette as a symbol of French friendship for the United States.

1791 Publishes *The Rights of Man* (part one), a sensational success.

1792 *The Rights of Man* (part two) published. Charges of sedition force flight to safety in France. Appointed to represent Calais in the French National Convention.

1793 Pleads for the life of King Louis XVI before the National Convention. Begins *The Age of Reason* and completes part one, but is arrested and imprisoned.

1794 Gains his release from Luxembourg Prison. *The Age of Reason* (part one) published.

1796   *The Age of Reason* (part two) published.

1802   Returns to the United States and settles in New York City.

1809   Dies on June 8, 1809, and is buried on his New Rochelle farm.

COMMON SENSE

Introduction

PERHAPS THE SENTIMENTS CONTAINED IN THE following pages are not *yet* sufficiently fashionable to procure them general favor; a long habit of not thinking a thing *wrong,* gives it a superficial appearance of being *right,* and raises at first a formidable outcry in defence of custom. But the tumult soon subsides. Time makes more converts than reason.

As a long and violent abuse of power is generally the Means of calling the right of it in question (and in matters too which might never have been thought of, had not the Sufferers been aggravated into the inquiry) and as the King of England hath undertaken in his *own Right,* to support the Parliament in what he calls *Theirs,* and as the good people of this country are grievously oppressed by the combination, they have an undoubted privilege to inquire into the pretensions of both, and equally to reject the usurpation of either.

In the following sheets, the author hath studiously avoided every thing which is personal among ourselves. Compliments as well as censure to individuals make no part thereof. The wise and the worthy need not the triumph of a pamphlet; and those whose sentiments are injudicious or unfriendly, will cease of themselves, unless too much pains are bestowed upon their conversion.

The cause of America is, in a great measure, the cause of all mankind. Many circumstances have, and will arise, which are not local, but universal, and through which the principles of all Lovers of Mankind are affected, and in the Event of which, their Affections are interested. The laying a Country desolate with Fire and Sword, declaring War against the natural rights of all Mankind, and extirpating the Defenders thereof from the Face of the Earth, is the Concern of every Man to whom Nature hath given the Power of feeling; of which Class, regardless of Party Censure, is

THE AUTHOR
PHILADELPHIA, *February 14, 1776*

OF THE ORIGIN AND DESIGN OF GOVERNMENT IN GENERAL, WITH CONCISE REMARKS ON THE ENGLISH CONSTITUTION

SOME WRITERS HAVE SO CONFOUNDED SOCIETY with government, as to leave little or no distinction between them; whereas they are not only different, but have different origins. Society is produced by our wants, and government by our wickedness; the former promotes our happiness *positively,* by uniting our affections; the latter *negatively,* by restraining our vices. The one encourages intercourse, the other creates distinctions. The first is a patron, the last is a punisher.

Society in every state is a blessing, but government, even in its best state, is but a necessary evil; in its worst state, an intolerable one; for when we suffer, or are exposed to the same miseries *by a government,* which we might expect in a country *without government,* our calamity is heightened by reflecting that we furnish the means by which we suffer. Government, like dress, is the badge of lost innocence: the palaces of kings are built on the ruins of the bowers of paradise. For, were the impulses of conscience clear, uniform, and irresistibly obeyed, man would need no other lawgiver; but that not being the case, he finds it necessary to surrender up a part of his property to furnish means for the protection of the rest; and this he is induced to do by the same prudence which, in every other case, advises him out of two evils to choose the least. *Wherefore,* security being the true design and end of government, it unanswerably follows, that whatever *form* thereof appears most likely to ensure it to us with the least expense and greatest benefit, is preferable to all others.

In order to give a clear and just idea of the design and end of government, let us suppose a small number of persons settled in some sequestered part of the earth, unconnected with the rest: they will then represent the first peopling of any country, or of the world. In this state of natural liberty, society will be their first thought. A thousand motives will excite them thereto; the strength of one man is so unequal to his wants, and his mind so unfitted for perpetual solitude, that he is soon obliged to seek assistance and relief of another, who in his turn requires the same. Four or five united would be able to raise a tolerable dwelling in the midst of a wilderness; but *one* man might labor out the common period of life without accomplishing anything: when he had felled his timber he could not remove it, nor erect it after it was removed; hunger in the mean time would urge him from his work, and every different want call him a different way. Disease, nay even misfortune, would be death; for though neither might be mortal, yet either would disable him from living, and reduce him to a state in which he might rather be said to perish than to die.

Thus necessity, like a gravitating power, would soon form our newly-arrived emigrants into society, the reciprocal blessings of which would supersede and render the obligations of law and government unnecessary while they remained perfectly just to each other: but as nothing but heaven is impregnable to vice, it will unavoidably happen, that in proportion as they surmount the first difficulties of emigration, which bound them together in a common cause, they will begin to relax in their duty and attachment to each other; and this remissness will point out the necessity of establishing some form of government to supply the defect of moral virtue.

Some convenient tree will afford them a State-House, under the branches of which the whole colony may assemble to deliberate on public matters. It is more than probable that their first laws will have the title only of REGULATIONS, and be enforced by no other penalty than public disesteem. In this first parliament every man, by natural right, will have a seat.

But as the colony increases, the public concerns will increase likewise, and the distance at which the members may be separated, will render it too inconvenient for all of them to meet on every occasion as at first, when their number was small, their habitations near, and the public concerns few and trifling. This will point out the convenience of their consenting to leave the legislative part to be managed by a select number chosen from the whole body, who are supposed to have the same concerns at stake which those have who appointed them, and who will act in the same manner as the whole body would were they present. If the colony continue increasing, it will become necessary to augment the number of representatives, and that the interest of every part of the colony may be attended to, it will be found best to divide the whole into convenient parts, each part sending its proper number; and that the *elected* might never form to themselves an interest separate from the *electors,* prudence will point out the propriety of having elections often; because as the *elected* might by that means return and mix again with the general body of the *electors* in a few months, their fidelity to the public will be secured by the prudent reflection of not making a rod for themselves. And as this frequent interchange will establish a common interest with every part of the community, they will mutually and naturally support each other, and on this (not on the unmeaning name of King) depends the *strength of government and the happiness of the governed.*

Here, then, is the origin and rise of government; namely, a mode rendered necessary by the moral virtue to govern the world; here too is the design and end of government, viz., freedom and security. And however our eyes may be dazzled with show, or our ears deceived by sound; however prejudice may warp our wills, or interest darken our understanding; the simple voice of nature and reason will say, it is right.

I draw my idea of the form of government from a principle in nature, which no art can overturn, viz., that the more simple anything is, the less liable it is to be disordered, and the easier repaired when disordered and with this maxim in view, I offer a few remarks on the so much boasted constitution of England. That it was noble for the dark and slavish times in which it was erected, is granted. When the world was overrun with tyranny the least remove therefrom was a glorious rescue. But that it is imperfect, subject to convulsions, and incapable of producing what it seems to promise, is easily demonstrated.

Absolute governments (though the disgrace of human nature) have this advantage with them, that they are simple; if the people suffer, they know the head from which their suffering springs, they know likewise the remedy, and are not bewildered by a variety of causes and cures. But the constitution of England is so exceedingly complex, that the nation may suffer for years together without being able to discover in which part the fault lies; some will say in one and some in another, and every political physician will advise a different medicine.

I know it is difficult to get over local or long standing prejudices, yet if we will suffer ourselves to examine the component parts of the English constitution, we shall find them to be the base remains of two ancient tyrannies, compounded with some new republican materials.

First.—The remains of monarchical tyranny in the person of the king.

Secondly.—The remains of aristocratical tyranny in the persons of the peers.

Thirdly.—The new republican materials in the persons of the commons, on whose virtue depends the freedom of England.

The two first, by being hereditary, are independent of the people; wherefore in a *constitutional sense* they contribute nothing towards the freedom of the state.

To say that the constitution of England is a *union* of three powers reciprocally *checking* each other, is farcical; either the words have no meaning, or they are flat contradictions.

To say that the commons is a check upon the king, presupposes two things:

First.—That the king is not to be trusted without being looked after, or in other words, that a thirst for absolute power is the natural disease of monarchy.

Secondly.—That the commons, by being appointed for that purpose, are either wiser or more worthy of confidence than the crown.

But as the same constitution which gives the commons a power to check the king by withholding the supplies, gives afterwards the king a power to check the commons by empowering him to reject their other bills, it again supposes that the king is wiser than those whom it has already supposed to be wiser than him. A mere absurdity!

There is something exceedingly ridiculous in the composition of monarchy; it first excludes a man from the means of information, yet empowers him to act in cases where the highest judgment is required. The state of a king shuts him from the world, yet the business of a king requires him to know it thoroughly; wherefore the different parts, by unnaturally opposing and destroying each other, prove the whole character to be absurd and useless.

Some writers have explained the English constitution thus: The king, say they, is one, the people another; the peers are a house in behalf of the king, the commons in behalf of the people. But this hath all the distinctions of a house divided against itself; and though the expressions be pleasantly arranged, yet when examined, they appear idle and ambiguous; and it will always happen, that the nicest construction that words are capable of, when applied to the description of something which either cannot exist or is too incomprehensible to be within the compass of description, will be words of sound only, and though they may amuse the ear, they cannot inform the mind, for this explanation includes a previous question, viz. *How came the king by a power which the people are afraid to trust, and always obliged to check?* Such a power could not be the gift of a wise people, neither can any power, *which needs checking,* be from God; yet the provision, which the constitution makes, supposes such a power to exist.

But the provision is unequal to the task; the means either cannot or will not accomplish the end, and the whole affair is a *felo de se;* for as the greater weight will always carry up the less, and as all the wheels of a machine are put in motion by one, it only remains to know which power in the constitution has the most weight, for that will govern; and though the others, or a part of them, may clog, or, as the phrase is, check the rapidity of its motion, yet so long as they cannot stop it, their endeavors will be ineffectual; the first moving power will at last have its way, and what it wants in speed, is supplied by time.

That the crown is this overbearing part in the English constitution, needs not be mentioned, and that it derives its whole consequence merely from being the giver of places and pensions, is self evident; wherefore, though we have been wise enough to shut and lock a door against absolute monarchy, we at the same time have been foolish enough to put the crown in possession of the key.

The prejudice of Englishmen in favor of their own government by kings, lords and commons, arises as much or more from national pride than reason. Individuals are undoubtedly safer in England than in some other countries, but the *will* of a king is as much the *law* of the land in Britain as in France, with this difference, that instead of proceeding directly from his mouth, it is handed to the people under the more formidable shape of an act of parliament. For the fate of Charles I hath only made kings more subtle—not more just.

Wherefore, laying aside all national pride and prejudice in favor of modes and forms, the plain truth is, that *it is wholly owing to the constitution of the people, and not to the constitution of the government,* that the crown is not as oppressive in England as in Turkey.

An inquiry into the *constitutional errors* in the English form of government is at this time highly necessary; for as we are never in a proper condition of doing justice to others, while we continue under the influence of some leading partiality, so neither are we capable of doing it to ourselves while we remain fettered by any obstinate prejudice. And as a man who is attached to a prostitute is unfitted to choose or judge of a wife, so any prepossession in favor of a rotten constitution of government will disable us from discerning a good one.

OF MONARCHY AND HEREDITARY SUCCESSION

MANKIND BEING ORIGINALLY EQUALS IN THE order of creation, the equality could only be destroyed by some subsequent circumstances; the distinctions of rich and poor, may in a great measure be accounted for, and that without having recourse to the harsh ill-sounding names of oppression and avarice. Oppression is often the *consequence,* but seldom or never the *means* of riches; and though avarice will preserve a man from being necessitously poor, it generally makes him too timorous to become wealthy.

But there is another and greater distinction, for which no truly natural or religious reason can be assigned, and that is, the distinction of men into KINGS and SUBJECTS. Male and female are the distinctions of nature, good and bad the distinction of heaven; but how a race of men came into the world so exalted above the rest, and distinguished like some new species, is worth enquiring into, and whether they are the means of happiness or of misery to mankind.

In the early ages of the world, according to the scripture chronology, there were no kings; the consequence of which was, there were no wars: it is the pride of kings which throws mankind into confusion. Holland without a king hath enjoyed more peace for this last century than any of the monarchical governments in Europe. Antiquity favors the same remark; for the quiet and rural lives of the first patriarchs hath a happy something in them, which vanishes away when we come to the history of Jewish royalty.

Government by kings was first introduced into the world by the Heathens, from whom the children of Israel copied the custom. It was the most prosperous invention the Devil ever set on foot for the promotion of idolatry. The Heathens paid divine honors to their deceased kings, and the Christian world hath improved on the plan, by doing the same to their living ones. How impious is the title of *sacred majesty* applied to a worm, who in the midst of his splendor is crumbling into dust!

As the exalting one man so greatly above the rest, cannot be justified on the equal rights of nature, so neither can it be defended on the authority of scripture; for the will of the Almighty, as declared by Gideon and the prophet Samuel, expressly disapproves of the government by kings. All anti-monarchical parts of scripture have been very smoothly glossed over in monarchical governments, but they undoubtedly merit the attention of countries which have their governments yet to form. *Render unto Cæsar the things which are Cæsar's* is the scripture doctrine of courts, yet it is no support of monarchical government, for the Jews at that time were without a king and in a state of vassalage to the Romans.

Near three thousand years passed away from the Mosaic account of the creation before the Jews, under a national delusion, requested a king. Till then their form of government (except in extraordinary cases where the Almighty interposed) was a kind of republic, administered by a judge and the elders of the tribe. Kings they had none, and it was held sinful to acknowledge any being under that title but the Lord of Hosts. And when a man seriously reflects on the idolatrous homage which is paid to the persons of kings he need not wonder that the Almighty, ever jealous of his honor, should disapprove a form of government which so impiously invades the prerogative of heaven.

Monarchy is ranked in scripture as one of the sins of the Jews, for which a curse in reserve is denounced against them. The history of that transaction is worth attending to.

The children of Israel being oppressed by the Midianites, Gideon marched against them with a small army, and victory, through the divine interposition, decided in his favor. The Jews, elate with success, and attributing it to the generalship of Gideon proposed making him a king, saying, *Rule thou over us, thou and thy son, and thy son's son.* Here was temptation in its fullest extent; not a kingdom only, but a hereditary one, but Gideon in the piety of his soul replied, *I will not rule over you, neither shall my son rule over you,* THE LORD SHALL RULE OVER YOU. Words need not be more explicit; Gideon doth not *decline* the honor, but denieth their right to give it; neither doth he compliment them with invented declarations of his thanks, but in the positive style of a prophet charges them with disaffection to their proper Sovereign, the King of Heaven.

About one hundred years after this, they fell again into the same error. The hankering which the Jews had for the idolatrous customs of the Heathens, is something exceedingly unaccountable; but so it was, that laying hold of the misconduct of Samuel's two sons, who were intrusted with some secular concerns, they came in an abrupt and clamorous manner to Samuel, saying, *Behold thou art old, and thy sons walk not in thy ways, now make us a king to judge us like all the other nations.* And here we cannot but observe that their motives were bad, viz. that they might be *like* unto other nations, *i.e.,* the Heathens, whereas their true glory lay in being as much *unlike* them as possible. *But the thing displeased Samuel when they said, Give us a king to judge us; and Samuel prayed unto the Lord, and the Lord said unto Samuel, Hearken unto the voice of the people in all that they say unto thee, for they have not rejected thee, but they have rejected me,* THAT I SHOULD NOT REIGN OVER THEM. *According to all the works which they have done since the day that I brought them up out of Egypt, even unto this day;*

*wherewith they have forsaken me, and served other Gods;
so do they also unto thee. Now therefore harken unto
their voice, howbeit, protest solemnly unto them, and
show them the manner of the king that shall reign over
them, i.e.,* not of any particular king, but the general manner of the kings of the earth, whom Israel
was so eagerly copying after. And notwithstanding
the great distance of time and difference of manners, the character is still in fashion. *And Samuel
told all the words of the Lord unto the people, that asked
of him a king. And he said, This shall be the manner
of the king that shall reign over you; he will take your
sons and appoint them for himself, for his chariots, and
to be his horsemen, and some shall run before his chariots* (this description agrees with the present mode
of impressing men) *and he will appoint him captains
over thousands, and captains over fifties and will set
them to ear his ground and to reap his harvest, and
to make his instruments of war, and instruments of his
chariots; and he will take your daughters to be confec-
tionaries, and to be cooks and to be bakers* (this
describes the expense and luxury as well as the
oppression of kings) *and he will take your fields and
your olive yards, even the best of them, and give them to
his servants; and he will take the tenth of your seed, and
of your vineyards, and give them to his officers and to
his servants* (by which we see that bribery, corruption, and favoritism, are the standing vices of
kings) *and he will take the tenth of your men servants,
and your maid servants, and your goodliest young men,
and your asses, and put them to his work; and he will
take the tenth of your sheep, and ye shall be his servants,*

and ye shall cry out in that day because of your king which ye shall have chosen, AND THE LORD WILL NOT HEAR YOU IN THAT DAY. This accounts for the continuation of monarchy; neither do the characters of the few good kings which have lived since, either sanctify the title, or blot out the sinfulness of the origin; the high encomium given of David takes no notice of him *officially as a king,* but only as a *man* after God's own heart. *Nevertheless the People refused to obey the voice of Samuel, and they said, Nay, but we will have a king over us, that we may be like all the nations, and that our king may judge us, and go out before us and fight our battles.* Samuel continued to reason with them, but to no purpose; he set before them their ingratitude, but all would not avail; and seeing them fully bent on their folly, he cried out, *I will call unto the Lord, and he shall send thunder and rain* (which was then a punishment, being in the time of wheat harvest) *that ye may perceive and see that your wickedness is great which ye have done in the sight of the Lord,* IN ASKING YOU A KING. *So Samuel called unto the Lord, and the Lord sent thunder and rain that day, and all the people greatly feared the Lord and Samuel. And all the people said unto Samuel, Pray for thy servants unto the Lord thy God that we die not, for* WE HAVE ADDED UNTO OUR SINS THIS EVIL, TO ASK A KING. These portions of scripture are direct and positive. They admit of no equivocal construction. That the Almighty hath here entered his protest against monarchical government is true, or the scripture is false. And a man hath good reason to believe, that there is as much of king-craft as priest-craft in withholding the scripture from the public in Popish countries. For monarchy in every instance is the Popery of government.

To the evil of monarchy we have added that of hereditary succession; and as the first is a degradation and lessening of ourselves, so the second, claimed as a matter of right, is an insult and imposition on posterity. For all men being originally equals, no *one* by *birth* could have a right to set up his own family in perpetual preference to all others forever, and though himself might deserve *some* decent degree of honors of his contemporaries, yet his descendants might be far too unworthy to inherit them. One of the strongest *natural* proofs of the folly of hereditary right of kings, is that nature disapproves it, otherwise she would not so frequently turn it into ridicule by giving mankind an *ass for a lion*.

Secondly, as no man at first could possess any other public honors than were bestowed upon him, so the givers of those honors could have no power to give away the right of posterity, and though they might say, "We choose you for *our* head," they could not, without manifest injustice to their children, say, "that your children and your children's children shall *reign* over *ours* for ever." Because such an unwise, unjust, unnatural compact might, perhaps, in the next succession put them under the government of a rogue or a fool. Most wise men in their private sentiments have ever treated hereditary right with contempt; yet it is one of those evils, which when once established is not easily removed; many submit from fear, others from superstition, and the more powerful part shares with the king the plunder of the rest.

This is supposing the present race of kings in the world to have had an honorable origin; whereas it is more than probable, that, could we take off the dark covering of antiquity and trace them to their first rise, we should find the first of them nothing better than the principal ruffian of some restless gang, whose savage manners or preeminence in subtilty obtained him the title of chief among plunderers; and who by increasing in power, and extending his depredations, overawed the quiet and defenceless to purchase their safety by frequent contributions. Yet his electors could have no idea of giving hereditary right to his descendants, because such a perpetual exclusion of themselves was incompatible with the free and unrestrained principles they professed to live by. Wherefore, hereditary succession in the early ages of monarchy could not take place as a matter of claim, but as something casual or complimental; but as few or no records were extant in those days, and traditionary history is stuffed with fables, it was very easy after the lapse of a few generations, to trump up some superstitious tale, conveniently timed, Mahomet like, to cram hereditary rights down the throats of the vulgar. Perhaps the disorders which threatened, or seemed to threaten, on the decease of a leader, and the choice of a new one (for elections among ruffians could not be very orderly) induced many at first to favor hereditary pretensions; by which means it happened, as it hath happened since, that what at first was submitted to as a convenience, was afterwards claimed as a right.

England, since the conquest, hath known some good monarchs, but groaned beneath a much larger number of bad ones; yet no man in his senses can say that their claim under William the Conqueror is a very honorable one. A French bastard landing with an armed banditti, and establishing himself king of England against the consent of the natives, is in plain terms a very paltry rascally original.—It certainly hath no divinity in it. However, it is needless to spend much time in exposing the folly of hereditary right, if there are any so weak as to believe it, let them promiscuously worship the ass and the lion, and welcome. I shall neither copy their humility nor disturb their devotion.

Yet I should be glad to ask, how they suppose kings came at first? The question admits but of three answers, viz. either by lot, by election, or by usurpation. If the first king was taken by lot, it establishes a precedent for the next, which excludes hereditary succession. Saul was by lot, yet the succession was not hereditary, neither does it appear from that transaction that there was any intention it ever should be. If the first king of any country was by election, that likewise establishes a precedent for the next; for to say, that the *right* of all future generations is taken away, by the act of the first electors, in their choice not only of a king, but of a family of kings forever, hath no parallel in or out of scripture but the doctrine of original sin, which supposes the free will of all men lost in Adam; and from such comparison, and it will admit of no other, hereditary succession can derive no glory. For as in Adam all sinned, and as in the first electors all men obeyed; as in the one all mankind were subjected to Satan, and in the other to Sovereignty; as our innocence was lost in the first, and our authority in the last; and as both disable us from re-assuming some former state and privilege, it unanswerably follows that original sin and hereditary succession are parallels. Dishonorable rank! Inglorious connection! Yet the most subtle sophist cannot produce a juster simile.

As to usurpation, no man can be so hardy as to defend it; and that William the Conqueror was an usurper is a fact not to be contradicted. The plain truth is, that the antiquity of English monarchy will not bear looking into.

But it is not so much the absurdity as the evil of hereditary succession which concerns mankind. Did it ensure a race of good and wise men it would have the seal of divine authority, but as it opens a door to the *foolish,* the *wicked,* and the *improper,* it hath in it the nature of oppression. Men who look upon themselves born to reign, and others to obey, soon grow insolent; selected from the rest of mankind, their minds are early poisoned by importance; and the world they act in differs so materially from the world at large, that they have but little opportunity of knowing its true interests, and when they succeed to the government are frequently the most ignorant and unfit of any throughout the dominions.

Another evil which attends hereditary succession is, that the throne is subject to be possessed by a minor at any age; all which time the regency under the cover of a king, have every opportunity and inducement to betray their trust. The same national misfortune happens, when a king, worn out with age and infirmity, enters the last stage of human weakness. In both these cases the public becomes the prey of every miscreant who can tamper successfully with the follies either of age or infancy.

The most plausible plea, which hath ever been offered in favor of hereditary succession, is that it preserves a nation from civil wars; and were this true, it would be weighty; whereas, it is the most bare-faced falsity ever imposed upon mankind. The whole history of England disowns the fact. Thirty kings and two minors have reigned in that distracted kingdom since the conquest, in which time there have been (including the Revolution) no less than eight civil wars and nineteen rebellions. Wherefore, instead of making for peace, it makes against it, and destroys the very foundation it seems to stand on.

The contest for monarchy and succession, between the houses of York and Lancaster, laid England in a scene of blood for many years. Twelve pitched battles, besides skirmishes and sieges, were fought between Henry and Edward.

Twice was Henry prisoner to Edward, who in his turn was prisoner to Henry. And so uncertain is the fate of war and the temper of a nation, when nothing but personal matters are the ground of a quarrel, that Henry was taken in triumph from a prison to a palace, and Edward obliged to fly from a palace to a foreign land; yet, as sudden transitions of temper are seldom lasting, Henry in his turn was driven from the throne, and Edward recalled to succeed him. The parliament always following the strongest side.

This contest began in the reign of Henry VI, and was not entirely extinguished till Henry VII, in whom the families were united. Including a period of sixty-seven years, viz. from 1422 to 1489.

In short, monarchy and succession have laid, not this or that kingdom only, but the world in blood and ashes. 'Tis a form of government which the word of God bears testimony against, and blood will attend it.

If we enquire into the business of a king, we shall find (and in some countries they have none) that after sauntering away their lives without pleasure to themselves or advantage to the nation, they withdraw from the scene, and leave their successors to tread the same useless and idle round. In absolute monarchies the whole weight of business, civil and military, lies on the king; the children of Israel in their request for a king urged this plea, "that he may judge us, and go out before us and fight our battles." But in countries where he is neither a judge nor a general, as in England, a man would be puzzled to know what *is* his business.

The nearer any government approaches to a republic, the less business there is for a king. It is somewhat difficult to find a proper name for the government of England. Sir William Meredith calls it a republic; but in its present state it is unworthy of the name, because the corrupt influence of the crown, by having all the places at its disposal, hath so effectually swallowed up the power, and eaten out the virtue of the house of commons (the republican part in the constitution) that the government of England is nearly as monarchical as that of France or Spain. Men fall out with names without understanding them. For it is the republican and not the monarchical part of the constitution of England which Englishmen glory in, viz., the liberty of choosing a house of commons from out of their own body—and it is easy to see that when republican virtue fails, slavery ensues. Why is the constitution of England sickly, but because monarchy hath poisoned the republic, the crown hath engrossed the commons?

In England a king hath little more to do than to make war and give away places; which, in plain terms, is to impoverish the nation and set it together by the ears. A pretty business indeed for a man to be allowed eight hundred thousand sterling a year for, and worshiped into the bargain! Of more worth is one honest man to society, and in the sight of God, than all the crowned ruffians that ever lived.

Thoughts on the Present State of American Affairs

In the following pages I offer nothing more than simple facts, plain arguments, and common sense; and have no other preliminaries to settle with the reader, than that he will divest himself of prejudice and prepossession, and suffer his reason and his feelings to determine for themselves; that he will put *on,* or rather that he will not put *off* the true character of a man, and generously enlarge his views beyond the present day.

Volumes have been written on the subject of the struggle between England and America. Men of all ranks have embarked in the controversy, from different motives, and with various designs: but all have been ineffectual, and the period of debate is closed. Arms, as a last resource, must decide the contest; the appeal was the choice of the king, and the continent hath accepted the challenge.

It has been reported of the late Mr. Pelham (who, though an able minister was not without his faults) that on his being attacked in the house of commons on the score that his measures were only of a temporary kind, replied, "*they will last my time.*" Should a thought so fatal and unmanly possess the colonies in the present contest, the name of ancestors will be remembered by future generations with detestation.

The sun never shone on a cause of greater worth. 'Tis not the affair of a city, a county, a province, or a kingdom, but of a continent—of at least one-eighth part of the habitable globe. 'Tis not the concern of a day, a year, or an age; posterity are virtually involved in the contest, and will be more or less affected even to the end of time, by the proceedings now. Now is the seed-time of continental union, faith and honor. The least fracture now will be like a name engraved with the point of a pin on the tender rind of a young oak; the wound will enlarge with the tree, and posterity read it in full grown characters.

By referring the matter from argument to arms, a new era for politics is struck; a new method of thinking hath arisen. All plans, proposals, &c., prior to the nineteenth of April, *i.e.,* to the commencement of hostilities, are like the almanacs of the last year; which, though proper then, are superseded and useless now. Whatever was advanced by the advocates on either side of the question then, terminated in one and the same point, viz., a union with Great Britain; the only difference between the parties was the method of effecting it; the one proposing force, the other friendship; but it hath so far happened that the first hath failed, and the second hath withdrawn her influence.

As much hath been said of the advantages of reconciliation, which, like an agreeable dream, hath passed away and left us as we were, it is but right that we should examine the contrary side of the argument, and enquire into some of the many material injuries which these colonies sustain, and always will sustain, by being connected with and dependent on Great-Britain. To examine that connection and dependence on the principles of nature and common sense; to see what we have to trust to, if separated, and what we are to expect, if dependent.

I have heard it asserted by some, that as America hath flourished under her former connection with Great Britain, that the same connection is necessary towards her future happiness, and will always have the same effect. Nothing can be more fallacious than this kind of argument. We may as well assert that because a child has thriven upon milk, that it is never to have meat, or that the first twenty years of our lives is to become a precedent for the next twenty. But even this is admitting more than is true, for I answer roundly, that America would have flourished as much, and probably much more, had no European power had anything to do with her. The commerce, by which she hath enriched herself, are the necessaries of life, and will always have a market while eating is the custom of Europe.

But she has protected us, say some. That she hath engrossed us is true, and defended the continent at our expense as well as her own, is admitted, and she would have defended Turkey from the same motives, viz., for the sake of trade and dominion.

Alas, we have been long led away by ancient prejudices, and made large sacrifices to superstition. We have boasted the protection of Great-Britain, without considering that her motive was *interest* not *attachment;* and that she did not protect us from *our enemies* on *our account,* but from *her enemies* on *her own account,* from those who had no quarrel with us on any *other account,* but who will always be our enemies on the *same account.* Let Britain waive her pretensions to the continent, or the continent throw off the dependence, and we should be at peace with France and Spain, were they at war with Britain. The miseries of Hanover last war ought to warn us against connections.

It hath lately been asserted in parliament, that the colonies have no relation to each other but through the parent country, *i.e.,* that Pennsylvania and the Jerseys, and so on for the rest, are sister colonies by the way of England; this is certainly a very round-about way of proving relationship, but it is the nearest and only true way of proving enemyship, if I may so call it. France and Spain never were, nor perhaps ever will be our enemies as *Americans,* but as our being the *subjects of Great Britain.*

But Britain is the parent country, say some. Then the more shame upon her conduct. Even brutes do not devour their young, nor savages make war upon their families; wherefore, the assertion, if true, turns to her reproach; but it happens not to be true, or only partly so, and the phrase *parent* or *mother country* hath been jesuitically adopted by the king and his parasites, with a low papistical design of gaining an unfair bias on the credulous weakness of our minds. Europe, and not England, is the parent country of America. This new world hath been the asylum for the persecuted lovers of civil and religious liberty from *every part* of Europe. Hither have they fled, not from the tender embraces of a mother, but from the cruelty of the monster; and it is so far true of England, that the same tyranny which drove the first emigrants from home, pursues their descendants still.

In this extensive quarter of the globe, we forget the narrow limits of three hundred and sixty miles (the extent of England) and carry our friendship on a larger scale; we claim brotherhood with every European Christian, and triumph in the generosity of the sentiment.

It is pleasant to observe by what regular gradations we surmount the force of local prejudice, as we enlarge our acquaintance with the world. A man born in any town in England divided into parishes, will naturally associate most with his fellow parishioners (because their interests in many cases will be common) and distinguish him by the name of *neighbour;* if he meet him but a few miles from home, he drops the narrow idea of a street, and salutes him by the name of *townsman;* if he travel out of the county, and meets him in any other, he forgets the minor divisions of street and town, and calls him *countryman, i.e., countyman;* but if in their foreign excursions they should associate in France or any other part of *Europe,* their local remembrance would be enlarged into that of *Englishmen.* And, by a just parity of reasoning, all Europeans meeting in America, or any other quarter of the globe, are *countrymen;* for England, Holland, Germany, or Sweden, when compared with the whole, stand in the same places on a larger scale, which the divisions of street, town and county do on the smaller ones; distinctions too limited for continental minds. Not one-third of the inhabitants, even of this province, are of English descent. Wherefore, I reprobate the phrase of parent or mother country applied to England only, as being false, selfish, narrow and ungenerous.

But admitting that we were all of English descent, what does it amount to? Nothing. Britain, being now an open enemy, extinguishes every other name and title; and to say that reconciliation is our duty, is truly farcical. The first king of England, of the present line (William the Conqueror) was a Frenchman, and half the peers of England are descendants from the same country; wherefore, by the same method of reasoning, England ought to be governed by France.

Much hath been said of the united strength of Britain and the colonies, that in conjunction they might bid defiance to the world. But this is mere presumption; the fate of war is uncertain, neither do the expressions mean anything; for this continent would never suffer itself to be drained of inhabitants, to support the British arms in either Asia, Africa, or Europe.

Besides, what have we to do with setting the world at defiance? Our plan is commerce, and that, well attended to, will secure us the peace and friendship of all Europe; because it is the interest of all Europe to have America a *free port*. Her trade will always be a protection, and her barrenness of gold and silver secure her from invaders.

I challenge the warmest advocate for reconciliation, to show a single advantage that this continent can reap by being connected with Great Britain. I repeat the challenge; not a single advantage is derived. Our corn will fetch its price in any market in Europe, and our imported goods must be paid for, buy them where we will.

But the injuries and disadvantages we sustain by that connection are without number, and our duty to mankind at large, as well as to ourselves, instructs us to renounce the alliance: Because any submission to or dependence on Great Britain tends directly to involve this continent in European wars and quarrels; and sets us at variance with nations who would otherwise seek our friendship, and against whom we have neither anger nor complaint. As Europe is our market for trade, we ought to form no partial connection with any part of it. It is the true interest of America to steer clear of European contentions, which she never can do while, by her dependence on Britain, she is made the make-weight in the scale of British politics.

Europe is too thickly planted with kingdoms to be long at peace, and whenever a war breaks out between England and any foreign power, the trade of America goes to ruin *because of her connection with Britain.* The next war may not turn out like the last, and should it not, the advocates for reconciliation now will be wishing for separation then, because neutrality in that case, would be a safer convoy than a man of war. Every thing that is right or natural pleads for separation. The blood of the slain, the weeping voice of nature cries, 'TIS TIME TO PART. Even the distance at which the Almighty hath placed England and America is a strong and natural proof that the authority of the one over the other was never the design of heaven. The time likewise at which the continent was discovered adds weight to the argument, and the manner in which it was peopled increases the force of it. The reformation was preceded by the discovery of America, as if the Almighty graciously meant to open a sanctuary to the persecuted in future years, when home should afford neither friendship nor safety.

The authority of Great-Britain over this continent is a form of government which sooner or later must have an end; and a serious mind can draw no true pleasure by looking forward under the painful and positive conviction, that what he calls "the present constitution" is merely temporary. As parents, we can have no joy, knowing that *this government* is not sufficiently lasting to ensure anything which we may bequeath to posterity, and by a plain method of argument, as we are running the next generation into debt, we ought to do the work of it, otherwise we use them meanly and pitifully. In order to discover the line of our duty rightly, we should take our children in our hand, and fix our station a few years further into life; that eminence will present a prospect which a few present fears and prejudices conceal from our sight.

Though I would carefully avoid giving unnecessary offence, yet I am inclined to believe, that all those who espouse the doctrine of reconciliation may be included within the following descriptions:

Interested men, who are not to be trusted; weak men, who *cannot* see; prejudiced men, who *will not* see; and a certain set of moderate men who think better of the European world than it deserves; and this last class, by an ill-judged deliberation, will be the cause of more calamities to this continent than all the other three.

It is the good fortune of many to live distant from the scene of sorrow; the evil is not sufficiently brought to *their* doors to *make* them feel the precariousness with which all American property is possessed. But let our imaginations transport us for a few moments to Boston; that seat of wretchedness will teach us wisdom, and instruct us to renounce a power in whom we can have no trust. The inhabitants of that unfortunate city, who but a few months ago were in ease and affluence, have now no other alternative than to stay and starve, or turn out to beg. Endangered by the fire of their friends if they continue within the city, and plundered by the soldiery if they leave it. In their present situation they are prisoners without the hope of redemption, and in a general attack for their relief, they would be exposed to the fury of both armies.

Men of passive tempers look somewhat lightly over the offences of Britain, and still hoping for the best, are apt to call out, "*Come, come, we shall be friends again for all this.*" But examine the passions and feelings of mankind, bring the doctrine of reconciliation to the touchstone of nature, and then tell me whether you can here-after love, honour, and faithfully serve the power that hath carried fire and sword into your land? If you cannot do all these, then you are only deceiving yourselves, and by your delay bringing ruin upon your posterity. Your future connection with Britain, whom you can neither love nor honor, will be forced and unnatural, and being formed only on the plan of present convenience, will in a little time fall into a relapse more wretched than the first. But if you say, you can still pass the violations over, then I ask, Hath your house been burnt? Hath your property been destroyed before your face? Are your wife and children destitute of a bed to lie on, or bread to live on? Have you lost a parent or a child by their hands,

and yourself the ruined and wretched survivor?
If you have not, then you are not a judge of
those who have. But if you have, and can still
shake hands with the murderers, then you are
unworthy the name of husband, father, friend, or
lover, and whatever may be your rank or title in
life, you have the heart of a coward, and the spirit
of a sycophant.

This is not inflaming or exaggerating matters,
but trying them by those feelings and affections
which nature justifies, and without which, we
should be incapable of discharging the social
duties of life, or enjoying the felicities of it. I mean
not to exhibit horror for the purpose of provok-
ing revenge, but to awaken us from fatal and
unmanly slumbers, that we may pursue determi-
nately some fixed object. It is not in the power of
Britain or of Europe to conquer America, if she
does not conquer herself by *delay* and *timidity*. The
present winter isn't worth an age if rightly
employed, but if lost or neglected the whole
continent will partake of the misfortune; and
there is no punishment which that man will not
deserve, be he who, or what, or where he will, that
may be the means of sacrificing a season so pre-
cious and useful.

It is repugnant to reason, to the universal
order of things, to all examples from former ages,
to suppose that this continent can longer remain
subject to any external power. The most sanguine
in Britain does not think so. The utmost stretch of
human wisdom cannot, at this time, compass a

plan short of separation, which can promise the continent even a year's security. Reconciliation is *now* a fallacious dream. Nature hath deserted the connection, and Art cannot supply her place. For, as Milton wisely expresses, "never can true reconcilement grow, where wounds of deadly hate have pierced so deep."

Every quiet method for peace hath been ineffectual. Our prayers have been rejected with disdain; and only tended to convince us that nothing flatters vanity, or confirms obstinacy in Kings more than repeated petitioning—and nothing hath contributed more than this very measure to make the kings of Europe absolute: Witness Denmark and Sweden. Wherefore, since nothing but blows will do, for God's sake, let us come to a final separation, and not leave the next generation to be cutting throats, under the violated unmeaning names of parent and child.

To say they will never attempt it again, is idle and visionary; we thought so at the repeal of the Stamp-Act, yet a year or two undeceived us: as well may we suppose that nations, which have been once defeated, will never renew the quarrel.

As to government matters, it is not in the power of Britain to do this continent justice: the business of it will soon be too weighty and intricate to be managed with any tolerable degree of convenience by a power so distant from us, and so very ignorant of us; for if they cannot conquer us, they cannot govern us. To be always running three or four thousand miles with a tale or a petition, waiting four or five months for an answer, which, when obtained, requires five or six more to explain it in, will in a few years be looked upon as folly and childishness—There was a time when it was proper, and there is a proper time for it to cease.

Small islands, not capable of protecting themselves, are the proper objects for kingdoms to take under their care; but there is something very absurd in supposing a continent to be perpetually governed by an island. In no instance hath nature made the satellite larger than its primary planet; and as England and America, with respect to each other, reverses the common order of nature, it is evident that they belong to different systems: England to Europe, America to itself.

I am not induced by motives of pride, party, or resentment to espouse the doctrine of separation and independence; I am clearly, positively, and conscientiously persuaded that it is the true interest of this continent to be so; that every thing short of *that* is mere patchwork; that it can afford no lasting felicity,—that it is leaving the sword to our children, and shrinking back at a time, when a little more, a little further, would have rendered this continent the glory of the earth.

As Britain hath not manifested the least inclination towards a compromise, we may be assured that no terms can be obtained worthy the acceptance of the continent, or any ways equal to the expense of blood and treasure we have been already put to.

The object contended for, ought always to bear some just proportion to the expense. The removal of North, or the whole detestable junto, is a matter unworthy the millions we have expended. A temporary stoppage of trade was an inconvenience which would have sufficiently balanced the repeal of all the acts complained of, had such repeals been obtained; but if the whole continent must take up arms, if every man must be a soldier, it is scarcely worth our while to fight against a contemptible ministry only. Dearly, dearly do we pay for the repeal of the acts, if that is all we fight for; for, in a just estimation, it is as great a folly to pay a Bunker-hill price for law as for land. As I have always considered the independency of this continent, as an event, which sooner or later must arrive, so from the late rapid progress of the continent to maturity, the event could not be far off. Wherefore, on the breaking out of hostilities, it was not worth the while to have disputed a matter which time would have fairly redressed, unless we meant to be in earnest; otherwise, it is like wasting an estate on a suit at law, to regulate the trespasses of a tenant whose lease is just expiring. No man was a warmer wisher for reconciliation than myself before the fatal nineteenth of April, 1775,[1] but the moment the event of that day was made known, I rejected the hardened, sullen-tempered Pharaoh of England forever; and disdain the wretch, that with the pretended title of FATHER OF HIS PEOPLE, can unfeelingly hear of their slaughter, and composedly sleep with their blood upon his soul.

But admitting that matters were now made up, what would be the event? I answer, the ruin of the continent. And that for several reasons:

First. The powers of governing still remaining in the hands of the king, he will have a negative over the whole legislation of the continent. And as he hath shown himself such an inveterate enemy to liberty, and discovered such a thirst for arbitrary power, is he, or is he not, a proper person to say to these colonies, "*You shall make no laws but what I please.*" And is there any inhabitant in America so ignorant as not to know, that I, according to what is called the *present constitution,* this continent can make no laws but what the king gives leave to; and is there any man so unwise as not to see, that (considering what has happened) he will suffer no law to be made here, but such as suits *his* purpose? We may be as effectually enslaved by the want of laws in America, as by submitting to laws made for us in England. After matters are made up (as it is called) can there be any doubt but the whole power of the crown will be exerted, to keep this continent as low and humble as possible? Instead of going forward we shall go backward, or be perpetually quarreling, or ridiculously petitioning.—We are already greater than the king wishes us to be, and will he not hereafter endeavor to make us less? To bring the matter to one point, Is the power who is jealous of our prosperity a proper power to govern us? Whoever says *No* to this question, is an *independent,* for independency means no more than this, whether we shall make our own laws, or whether the king, the greatest enemy which this continent hath or can have, shall tell us, *"there shall be no laws but such as I like."*

But the king, you will say, has a negative in England; the people there can make no laws without his consent. In point of right and good order, there is something very ridiculous, that a youth of twenty-one (which hath often happened) shall say to several millions of people, older and wiser than himself, I forbid this or that act of yours to be law. But in this place I decline this sort of reply, though I will never cease to expose the absurdity of it; and only answer, that England being the king's residence and America not, makes quite another case. The king's negative *here* is ten times more dangerous and fatal than it can be in England, for *there* he will scarcely refuse his consent to a bill for putting England into as strong a state of defence as possible, and in America he would never suffer such a bill to be passed.

America is only a secondary object in the system of British politics—England consults the good of *this* country no further than it answers her *own* purpose. Wherefore, her own interest leads her to suppress the growth of *ours* in every case which doth not promote her advantage, or in the least interferes with it. A pretty state we should soon be in under such a second-hand government, considering what has happened! Men do not change from enemies to friends by the alteration of a name; and in order to show that reconciliation *now* is a dangerous doctrine, I affirm, *that it would be policy in the king at this time, to repeal the acts, for the sake of reinstating himself in the government of the provinces;* in order that HE MAY ACCOMPLISH BY CRAFT AND SUBTLETY, IN THE LONG RUN, WHAT HE CANNOT DO BY FORCE AND VIOLENCE IN THE SHORT ONE. Reconciliation and ruin are nearly related.

Secondly, That as even the best terms, which we can expect to obtain, can amount to no more than a temporary expedient, or a kind of government by guardianship, which can last no longer than till the colonies come of age, so the general face and state of things, in the interim, will be unsettled and unpromising. Emigrants of property will not choose to come to a country whose form of government hangs but by a thread, and which is every day tottering on the brink of commotion and disturbance; and numbers of the present inhabitants would lay hold of the interval to dispose of their effects, and quit the continent.

But the most powerful of all arguments is, that nothing but independence, *i.e.*, a continental form of government, can keep the peace of the continent and preserve it inviolate from civil wars. I dread the event of a reconciliation with Britain now, as it is more than probable that it will be followed by a revolt somewhere or other, the consequences of which may be far more fatal than all the malice of Britain.

Thousands are already ruined by British barbarity. Thousands more will probably suffer the same fate. Those men have other feelings than us who have nothing suffered. All they *now* possess is liberty; what they before enjoyed is sacrificed to its service, and having nothing more to lose, they disdain submission. Besides, the general temper of the colonies towards a British government, will be like that of a youth who is nearly out of his time; they will care very little about her. And a government which cannot preserve the peace, is no government at all, and in that case we pay our money for nothing; and pray what is it that Britain can do, whose power will be wholly on paper, should a civil tumult break out the very day after reconciliation? I have heard some men say, many of whom I believe spoke without thinking, that they dreaded an independence, fearing that it would produce civil wars. It is but seldom that our first thoughts are truly correct, and that is the case here; for there is ten times more to dread from a patched up connection than from independence. I make the sufferer's case my own, and I protest, that were I driven from house and home, my property destroyed, and my circumstances ruined, that as a man, sensible of injuries, I could never relish the doctrine of reconciliation, or consider myself bound thereby.

The colonies have manifested such a spirit of good order and obedience to continental government, as is sufficient to make every reasonable person easy and happy on that head. No man can assign the least pretense for his fears, on any other grounds, than such as are truly childish and ridiculous, viz., that one colony will be striving for superiority over another.

Where there are no distinctions there can be no superiority; perfect equality affords no temptation. The republics of Europe are all (and we may say always) in peace: Holland and Switzeland are without wars, foreign or domestic; monarchical governments, it is true, are never long at rest: the crown itself is a temptation to enterprising ruffians at home; and that degree of pride and insolence ever attendant on legal authority, swells into a rupture with foreign powers, in instances where a republican government, by being formed on more natural principles, would negotiate the mistake.

If there is any true cause of fear respecting independence, it is because no plan is yet laid down. Men do not see their way out—Wherefore, as an opening into that business, I offer the following hints; at the same time modestly affirming, that I have no other opinion of them myself, than that they may be the means of giving rise to something better. Could the straggling thoughts of individuals be collected, they would frequently form materials for wise and able men to improve into useful matter.

Let the assemblies be annual, with a President only. The representation more equal. Their business wholly domestic, and subject to the authority of a Continental Congress.

Let each colony be divided into six, eight, or ten, convenient districts, each district to send a proper number of delegates to Congress, so that each colony sends at least thirty. The whole number in Congress will be at least three hundred and ninety. Each Congress to sit . . . and to choose a president by the following method: When the delegates are met, let a colony be taken from the whole thirteen colonies by lot, after which, let the whole Congress choose (by ballot) a president from out of the delegates of that province. In the next Congress, let a colony be taken by lot from twelve only, omitting that colony from which the president was taken in the former Congress, and so proceeding on till the whole thirteen shall have had their proper rotation. And in order that nothing may pass into a law but what is satisfactorily just, not less than three-fifths of the congress to be called a majority. He that will promote discord, under a government so equally formed as this, would have joined Lucifer in his revolt.

But as there is a peculiar delicacy, from whom or in what manner this business must first arise, and as it seems most agreeable and consistent that it should come from some intermediate body between the governed and the governors, that is, between the Congress and the people, let a CONTINENTAL CONFERENCE be held, in the following manner, and for the following purpose:

A committee of twenty-six members of Congress, viz. two for each colony. Two members from each house of assembly, or Provincial convention; and five representatives of the people at large, to be chosen in the capital city or town of each province, for and in behalf of the whole province, by as many qualified voters as shall think proper to attend from all parts of the province for that purpose; or, if more convenient, the representatives may be chosen in two or three of the most populous parts thereof. In this conference, thus assembled, will be united, the two grand principles of business, *knowledge* and *power*. The members of Congress, Assemblies, or Conventions, by having had experience in national concerns, will be able and useful counsellors, and the whole, being empowered by the people, will have a truly legal authority.

The conferring members being met, let their business be to frame a CONTINENTAL CHARTER, or Charter of the United Colonies; (answering to what is called the Magna Charta of England) fixing the number and manner of choosing members of Congress, and members of Assembly, with their date of sitting, and drawing the line of business and jurisdiction between them: (Always remembering, that our strength is continental, not provincial:) Securing freedom and property to all men, and above all things, the free exercise of religion, according to the dictates of conscience; with such other matter as is necessary for a charter to contain. Immediately after which, the said conference to dissolve, and the bodies which shall be chosen conformable to the said charter, to be the legislators and governors of this continent for the time being: Whose peace and happiness, may God preserve, Amen.

Should any body of men be hereafter delegated for this or some similar purpose, I offer them the following extracts from that wise observer on governments, *Dragonetti.* "The science," says he, "of the politician consists in fixing the true point of happiness and freedom. Those men would deserve the gratitude of ages, who should discover a mode of government that contained the greatest sum of individual happiness, with the least national expense."—*Dragonetti on Virtue and Rewards.*

But where, say some, is the King of America? I'll tell you, friend, he reigns above, and doth not make havoc of mankind like the Royal brute of Britain. Yet that we may not appear to be defective even in earthly honors, let a day be solemnly set apart for proclaiming the charter; let it be brought forth, placed on the divine law, the word of God; let a crown be placed thereon, by which the world may know, that so far as we approve of monarchy, that in America THE LAW IS KING. For as in absolute governments the king is law, so in free countries the law ought to be king; and there ought to be no other. But lest any ill use should afterwards arise, let the crown at the conclusion of the ceremony be demolished and scattered among the people whose right it is.

A government of our own is our natural right: and when a man seriously reflects on the precariousness of human affairs, he will become convinced that it is infinitely wiser and safer to form a constitution of our own, in a cool deliberate manner, while we have it in our power, than to trust such an interesting event to time and chance. If we omit it now, some Massaniello[2] may hereafter arise, who, laying hold of popular disquietudes, may collect together the desperate and the discontented, and by assuming to themselves the powers of government, may sweep away the liberties of the continent like a deluge. Should the government of America return again into the hands of Britain, the tottering situation of things will be a temptation for some desperate adventurer to try his fortune; and in such a case, what relief can Britain give? Ere she could hear the news, the fatal business might be done; and ourselves suffering like the wretched Britons under the oppression of the conqueror. Ye that oppose independence now, ye know not what ye do; ye are opening a door to eternal tyranny, by keeping vacant the seat of government.

There are thousands and tens of thousands who would think it glorious to expel from the continent that barbarous and hellish power which hath stirred up the Indians and Negroes to destroy us; the cruelty hath a double guilt; it is dealing brutally by us and treacherously by them. To talk of friendship with those in whom our reason forbids us to have faith, and our affections wounded through a thousand pores instruct us to detest, is madness and folly. Every day wears out the little remains of kindred between us and them; and can there be any reason to hope that as the relationship expires the affection will increase, or that we shall agree better when we have ten times more and greater concerns to quarrel over than ever?

Ye that tell us of harmony and reconciliation, can ye restore to us the time that is passed? Can ye give to prostitution its former innocence? Neither can ye reconcile Britain and America. The last cord now is broken; the people of England are presenting addresses against us. There are injuries which nature cannot forgive; she would cease to be nature if she did. As well can the lover forgive the ravisher of his mistress, as the continent forgive the murders of Britain. The Almighty hath implanted in us these unextinguishable feelings for good and wise purposes. They are the guardians of his image in our hearts. They distinguish us from the herd of common animals. The social compact would dissolve and justice be extirpated from the earth, or have only a casual existence, were we callous to the touches of affection. The robber and the murderer would often escape unpunished, did not the injuries which our tempers sustain, provoke us into justice.

O ye that love mankind! Ye that dare oppose, not only the tyranny, but the tyrant, stand forth! Every spot of the old world is overrun with oppression. Freedom hath been hunted round the globe. Asia and Africa have long expelled her, Europe regards her like a stranger, and England hath given her warning to depart. O! receive the fugitive, and prepare in time an asylum for mankind.

---

[1] Massacre at Lexington

[2] Thomas Aniello, otherwise Massaniello, a fisherman of Naples, who after spiriting up his countrymen in the public marketplace, against the oppression of the Spaniards, to whom the place was then subject, prompted them to revolt, and in the space of a day became King.

Of the Present Ability of America, with Some Miscellaneous Reflections

I HAVE NEVER MET WITH A MAN, EITHER IN England or America, who hath not confessed his opinion that a separation between the countries would take place one time or other: and there is no instance, in which we have shown less judgment, than in endeavoring to describe what we call the ripeness or fitness of the Continent for independence.

As all men allow the measure, and vary only in their opinion of the time, let us, in order to remove mistakes, take a general survey of things, and endeavor, if possible, to find out the *very* time. But we need not go far, the inquiry ceases at once, for the *time hath found us.* The general concurrence, the glorious union of all things proves the fact.

It is not in numbers, but in unity, that our great strength lies; yet our present numbers are sufficient to repel the force of all the world. The Continent, hath, at this time, the largest body of armed and disciplined men of any power under

Heaven; and is just arrived at that pitch of strength, in which no single colony is able to support itself, and the whole when united can accomplish the matter, and either more or less than this might be fatal in its effects. Our land force is already sufficient, and as to naval affairs, we cannot be insensible, that Britain would never suffer an American man of war to be built while the continent remained in her hands. Wherefore, we should be no forwarder an hundred years hence in that branch than we are now; but the truth is, we should be less so, because the timber of the country is every day diminishing, and that which will remain at last will be far off or difficult to procure.

Were the continent crowded with inhabitants, her sufferings under the present circumstances would be intolerable. The more seaport towns we had, the more should we have both to defend and to lose. Our present numbers are so happily proportioned to our wants, that no man need be idle. The diminution of trade affords an army, and the necessities of an army create a new trade. Debts we have none: and whatever we may contract on this account will serve as a glorious memento of our virtue. Can we but leave posterity with a settled form of government, an independent constitution of its own, the purchase at any price will be cheap. But to expend millions for the sake of getting a few vile acts repealed, and routing the present ministry only, is unworthy the charge, and is using posterity with the utmost cruelty; because it is leaving them the great work to do, and a debt upon their backs from which they derive no advantage. Such a thought is unworthy a man of honor, and is the true characteristic of a narrow heart and a peddling politician.

The debt we may contract doth not deserve our regard, if the work be but accomplished. No nation ought to be without a debt. A national debt is a national bond; and when it bears no interest, is in no case a grievance. Britain is oppressed with a debt of upwards of one hundred and forty millions sterling, for which she pays upwards of four millions interest. And as a compensation for her debt, she has a large navy; America is without a debt, and without a navy; yet for the twentieth part of the English national debt, could have a navy as large again. The navy of England is not worth, at this time, more than three millions and a half sterling.

The following calculations are given as a proof that the above estimation of the navy is a just one. *(See Entick's Naval History, Intro, page 56.)*

The charge of building a ship of each rate, and furnishing her with masts, yards, sails, and rigging, together with a proportion of eight months boatswain's and carpenter's sea-stores, as calculated by Mr. Burchett, Secretary to the navy, is as follows:

For a ship of 100 guns	£35,553
90	29,886
80	23,638
70	17,785
60	14,197
50	10,606
40	7,758
30	5,846
20	3,710

And from hence it is easy to sum up the value, or cost rather, of the whole British navy, which in the year 1757 when it was at its greatest glory, consisted of the following ships and guns:

Ships	Guns	Cost of one	Cost of all
6	100	£35,553	£213,318
12	90	29,886	358,632
12	80	23,638	283,656
43	70	17,785	764,755
35	60	14,197	496,895
40	50	10,606	424,240
45	40	7,758	344,110
58	20	3,710	215,180
85	Sloops, bombs, and fireships, one with another	2,000	170,000
		Cost	3,270,786
	Remains for guns		229,214
			3,500,000

No country on the globe is so happily situated, or so internally capable of raising a fleet as America. Tar, timber, iron, and cordage are her natural produce. We need go abroad for nothing. Whereas the Dutch, who make large profits by hiring out their ships of war to the Spaniards and Portuguese, are obliged to import most of the materials they use. We ought to view the building a fleet as an article of commerce, it being the natural manufacture of this country. It is the best money we can lay out. A navy when finished is worth more than it cost: and is that nice point in national policy, in which commerce and protection are united. Let us build; if we want them not, we can sell; and by that means replace our paper currency with ready gold and silver.

In point of manning a fleet, people in general run into great errors; it is not necessary that one-fourth part should be sailors. The Terrible Privateer, Captain Death, stood the hottest engagement of any ship last war, yet had not twenty sailors on board, though her complement of men was upwards of two hundred. A few able and social sailors will soon instruct a sufficient number of active landsmen in the common work of a ship. Wherefore, we never can be more capable to begin on maritime matters than now, while our timber is standing, our fisheries blocked up, and our sailors and shipwrights out of employ. Men of war, of seventy and eighty guns, were built forty years ago in New-England, and why not the same now? Ship-building is America's greatest pride, and in which she will, in time, excel the whole world. The great empires of the east are mostly inland, and consequently excluded from the possibility of rivaling her. Africa is in a state of barbarism; and no power in Europe hath either such an extent of coast, or such an internal supply of materials. Where nature hath given the one, she hath withheld the other; to America only hath she been liberal of both. The vast empire of Russia is almost shut out from the sea; wherefore, her boundless forests, her tar, iron, and cordage are only articles of commerce.

In point of safety, ought we to be without a fleet? We are not the little people now which we were sixty years ago; at that time we might have trusted our property in the streets, or fields rather; and slept securely without locks or bolts to our doors or windows. The case is now altered, and our methods of defence ought to improve with our increase of property. A common pirate, twelve months ago, might have come up the Delaware, and laid the city of Philadelphia under instant contribution for what sum he pleased; and the same might have happened to other places. Nay, any daring fellow, in a brig of fourteen or sixteen guns, might have robbed the whole Continent, and carried off half a million of money. These are circumstances which demand our attention, and point out the necessity of naval protection.

Some, perhaps, will say, that after we have made it up with Britain, she will protect us. Can they be so unwise as to mean, that she will keep a navy in our harbours for that purpose? Common sense will tell us that the power which hath endeavored to subdue us, is of all others the most improper to defend us. Conquest may be effected under the pretense of friendship; and ourselves, after a long and brave resistance, be at last cheated into slavery. And if her ships are not to be admitted into our harbours, I would ask, how is she to protect us? A navy three or four thousand miles off can be of little use, and on sudden emergencies, none at all. Wherefore, if we must hereafter protect ourselves, why not do it for ourselves? Why do it for another?

The English list of ships of war is long and formidable, but not a tenth part of them are at any one time fit for service, numbers of them are not in being; yet their names are pompously continued in the list if only a plank be left of the ship; and not a fifth part of such as are fit for service can be spared on any one station at one time. The East, and West Indies, Mediterranean, Africa, and other parts of the world, over which Britain extends her claim, make large demands upon her navy. From a mixture of prejudice and inattention, we have contracted a false notion respecting the navy of England, and have talked as if we should have the whole of it to encounter at once, and, for that reason, supposed that we must have one as large; which not being instantly practicable, has been made use of by a set of disguised Tories to discourage our beginning thereon. Nothing can be further from truth than this; for if

America had only a twentieth part of the naval force of Britain, she would be by far an over match for her; because, as we neither have, nor claim any foreign dominion, our whole force would be employed on our own coast, where we should, in the long run, have two to one the advantage of those who had three or four thousand miles to sail over before they could attack us, and the same distance to return in order to refit and recruit. And although Britain, by her fleet, hath a check over our trade to Europe, we have as large a one over her trade to the West-Indies, which by laying in the neighbourhood of the Continent is entirely at its mercy.

Some method might be fallen on to keep up a naval force in time of peace, if we should not judge it necessary to support a constant navy. If premiums were to be given to merchants to build and employ in their service, ships mounted with twenty, thirty, forty or fifty guns, (the premiums to be in proportion to the loss of bulk to the merchants) fifty or sixty of those ships with a few guard-ships on constant duty, would keep up a sufficient navy, and that without burdening ourselves with the evil so loudly complained of in England, of suffering their fleet in time of peace to lie rotting in the docks. To unite the sinews of commerce and defence is sound policy; for when our strength and our riches play into each other's hand, we need fear no external enemy.

In almost every article of defence we abound. Hemp flourishes even to rankness, so that we need not want cordage. Our iron is superior to that of other countries. Our small arms equal to any in the world. Cannon we can cast at pleasure. Saltpeter and gunpowder we are every day producing. Our knowledge is hourly improving. Resolution is our inherent character, and courage hath not yet forsaken us. Wherefore, what is it that we want? Why is it that we hesitate? From Britain we can expect nothing but ruin. If she is once admitted to the government of America again, this Continent will not be worth living in. Jealousies will be always arising, insurrections will be constantly happening; and who will go forth to quell them? Who will venture his life to reduce his own countrymen to a foreign obedience? The difference between Pennsylvania and Connecticut, respecting some unlocated lands, shows the insignificance of a British government, and fully proves that nothing but continental authority can regulate Continental matters.

Another reason why the present time is preferable to all others, is that the fewer our numbers are, the more land there is yet unoccupied, which, instead of being lavished by the king on his worthless dependents, may be hereafter applied, not only to the discharge of the present debt, but to the constant support of government. No nation under heaven hath such an advantage as this.

The infant state of the Colonies, as it is called, so far from being against, is an argument in favor of independence. We are sufficiently numerous, and were we more so we might be less united. It is a matter worthy of observation, that the more a country is peopled, the smaller their armies are. In military numbers, the ancients far exceeded the moderns: and the reason is evident, for trade being the consequence of population, men became too much absorbed thereby to attend to anything else. Commerce diminishes the spirit both of patriotism and military defence. And history sufficiently informs us, that the bravest achievements were always accomplished in the non-age of a nation. With the increase of commerce England hath lost its spirit. The city of London, notwithstanding its numbers, submits to continued insults with the patience of a coward. The more men have to lose, the less willing they are to venture. The rich are in general slaves to fear, and submit to courtly power with the trembling duplicity of a spaniel.

Youth is the seed time of good habits, as well in nations as in individuals. It might be difficult, if not impossible, to form the Continent into one government half a century hence. The vast variety of interests, occasioned by an increase of trade and population, would create confusion. Colony would be against colony. Each being able, might scorn each other's assistance; and while the proud and foolish gloried in their little distinctions, the wise would lament that the union had not been formed before. Wherefore, the *present time* is the *true time* for establishing it. The intimacy which is contracted in infancy, and the friendship which is formed in misfortune, are of all others, the most lasting and unalterable. Our present union is marked with both these characters; we are young, and we have been distressed; but our concord hath withstood our troubles, and fixes a memorable era for posterity to glory in.

The present time, likewise, is that peculiar time which never happens to a nation but once, viz., the time of forming itself into a government. Most nations have let slip the opportunity, and by that means have been compelled to receive laws from their conquerors, instead of making laws for themselves. First, they had a king, and then a form of government; whereas the articles or charter of government, should be formed first, and men delegated to execute them afterwards: but from the errors of other nations, let us learn wisdom, and lay hold of the present opportunity—*To begin government at the right end.*

When William the Conqueror subdued England, he gave them law at the point of the sword; and until we consent that the seat of government in America be legally and authoritatively occupied, we shall be in danger of having it filled by some fortunate ruffian, who may treat us in the same manner, and then, where will be our freedom? where our property?

As to religion, I hold it to be the indispensible duty of all governments to protect all conscientious professors thereof, and I know of no other business which government hath to do therewith. Let a man throw aside that narrowness of soul, that selfishness of principle, which the niggards of all professions are so unwilling to part with, and he will be at once delivered of his fears on that head. Suspicion is the companion of mean souls, and the bane of all good society. For myself, I fully and conscientiously believe, that it is the will of the Almighty, that there should be a diversity of religious opinions among us: it affords a larger field for our Christian kindness. Were we all of one way of thinking, our religious dispositions would want matter for probation, and on this liberal principle, I look on the various denominations among us, to be like children of the same family, differing only in what is called their Christian names.

In page thirty-five,[1] I threw out a few thoughts on the propriety of a Continental Charter, (for I only presume to offer hints, not plans) and in this place I take the liberty of rementioning the subject, by observing, that a charter is to be understood as a bond of solemn obligation, which the whole enters into, to support the right of every separate part, whether of religion, personal freedom, or property. A firm bargain and a right reckoning make long friends.

In a former page I likewise mentioned the necessity of a large and equal representation; and there is no political matter which more deserves our attention. A small number of electors, or a small number of representatives, are equally dangerous. But if the number of the representatives be not only small, but unequal, the danger is increased. As an instance of this, I mention the following: when the associators petition was before the House of Assembly of Pennsylvania, twenty-eight members only were present; all the Bucks County members, being eight, voted against it, and had seven of the Chester members done the same, this whole province had then been governed by two counties only; and this danger it is always exposed to. The unwarrantable stretch, likewise, which that house made in their last sitting, to gain an undue authority over the Delegates of that province, ought to warn the people at large how they trust power out of their own hands. A set of instructions for their Delegates were put together, which in point of sense and business would have dishonored a school-boy, and after being approved of by a *few,* a *very few,* without doors, were carried into the House, and there passed *in behalf of the whole colony;* whereas, did the whole colony know with what ill will that House had entered on some necessary public measures, they would not hesitate a moment to think them unworthy of such a trust.

Immediate necessity makes many things convenient, which if continued would grow into oppressions. Expedience and right are different things. When the calamities of America required a consultation, there was no method so ready, or at that time so proper, as to appoint persons from the several Houses of Assembly for that purpose; and the wisdom with which they have proceeded hath preserved this continent from ruin. But as it is more than probable that we shall never be without a CONGRESS, every well-wisher to good order must own, that the mode for choosing members of that body, deserves consideration. And I put it as a question to those who make a study of mankind, whether *representation and election* is not too great a power for one and the same body of men to possess? Whenever we are planning for posterity we ought to remember that virtue is not hereditary.

It is from our enemies that we often gain excellent maxims, and are frequently surprised into reason by their mistakes. Mr. Cornwall (one of the Lords of the Treasury) treated the petition of the New York Assembly with contempt, because *that* house, he said, consisted but of twenty-six members, which trifling number, he argued, could not with decency be put for the whole. We thank him for his involuntary honesty.[2]

To CONCLUDE, however strange it may appear to some, however unwilling they may be to think so, matters not, but many strong and striking reasons may be given, to show that nothing can settle our affairs so expeditiously as an open and determined declaration for independence. Some of which are,

First.—It is the custom of nations, when any two are at war, for some other powers, not engaged in the quarrel, to step in as mediators, and bring about the preliminaries of a peace: but while America calls herself the subject of Great-Britain no power, however well disposed she may be, can offer her mediation. Wherefore, in our present state, we may quarrel on forever.

Secondly.—It is unreasonable to suppose that France or Spain will give us any kind of assistance, if we mean only to make use of that assistance for the purpose of repairing the breach, and strengthening the connection between Britain and America; because, those powers would be sufferers by the consequences.

Thirdly.—While we profess ourselves the subjects of Britain, we must, in the eyes of foreign nations, be considered as rebels. The precedent is somewhat dangerous to *their peace,* for men to be in arms under the name of subjects; we, on the spot, can solve the paradox: but to unite resistance and subjection, requires an idea much too refined for common understanding.

Fourthly.—Were a manifesto to be published and dispatched to foreign courts, setting forth the miseries we have endured, and the peaceful methods which we have ineffectually used for redress; declaring at the same time, that not being able, any longer, to live happily or safely under the cruel disposition of the British court, we had been driven to the necessity of breaking off all connection with her; at the same time, assuring all such courts of our peaceable disposition towards them, and of our desire of entering into trade with them. Such a memorial would produce more good effects to this Continent than if a ship were freighted with petitions to Britain.

Under our present denomination of British subjects, we can neither be received nor heard abroad: the custom of all courts is against us, and will be so, until, by an independence, we take rank with other nations.

These proceedings may at first appear strange and difficult; but like all other steps which we have already passed over, will in a little time become familiar and agreeable; and, until an independence is declared, the Continent will feel itself like a man who continues putting off some unpleasant business from day to day, yet knows it must be done, hates to set about it, wishes it over, and is continually haunted with the thoughts of its necessity.

---

[1] Page 45 of this edition. [PUBLISHER'S NOTE]

[2] Those who would fully understand of what great consequence a large and equal representation is to a State, should read Burgh's *Political Disquisitions.*

Appendix

Since the publication of the first edition of this pamphlet, or rather, on the same day on which it came out, the King's speech made its appearance in this city. Had the spirit of prophecy directed the birth of this production, it could not have brought it forth at a more seasonable juncture, or at a more necessary time. The bloody-mindedness of the one, shows the necessity of pursuing the doctrine of the other. Men read by way of revenge: and the speech, instead of terrifying, prepared a way for the manly principles of Independence.

Ceremony, and even silence, from whatever motives they may arise, have a hurtful tendency when they give the least degree of countenance to base and wicked performances; wherefore, if this maxim be admitted, it naturally follows, that the king's speech, as being a piece of finished villainy, deserved and still deserves a general execration, both by the Congress and the people. Yet, as the domestic tranquility of a nation depends greatly on the *chastity* of what may properly be called NATIONAL MANNERS, it is often better to pass some things over in silent disdain, than to make use of such new methods of dislike, as might introduce the least innovation on that guardian of our peace and safety. And, perhaps, it is chiefly owing to this prudent delicacy, that the king's speech hath not before now suffered a public execution. The Speech if it may be called one, is nothing better than a willful, audacious libel against the truth, the common good, and the existence of mankind; and is a formal and pompous method of offering up human sacrifices to the pride of tyrants. But this general massacre of mankind is one of the privileges and the certain consequences of Kings; *for* as nature knows them *not*, they know *not her*, and although they are beings of our *own* creating, they know not *us*, and are become the gods of their creators. The speech hath one good quality, which is, that it is not calculated to deceive, neither can we, if we would, be deceived by it. Brutality and tyranny appear on the face of it. It leaves us at no loss; and every line convinces, even in the moment of reading, that He, who hunts the woods for prey, the naked and untutored Indian is less Savage than the King of Britain.

Sir John Dalrymple, the putative father of a whining Jesuitical piece, fallaciously called, *The Address of the people of* ENGLAND *to the inhabitants of* AMERICA, hath perhaps, from a vain supposition that the people *here* were to be frightened at the pomp and description of a king, given (though very unwisely on his part) the real character of the present one: "But," says this writer, "if you are inclined to pay compliments to an administration, which we do not complain of," (meaning the Marquis of Rockingham's at the repeal of the Stamp Act) "it is very unfair in you to withhold them from that prince, *by whose* NOD ALONE *they were permitted to do anything.*" This is toryism with a witness! Here is idolatry even without a mask; and he who can calmly hear and digest such doctrine, hath forfeited his claim to rationality; is an apostate from the order of manhood, and ought to be considered—as one, who hath not only given up the proper dignity of man, but sunk himself beneath the rank of animals and contemptibly crawls through the world like a worm.

However, it matters very little now, what the King of England either says or does; he hath wickedly broken through every moral and human obligation, trampled nature and conscience beneath his feet; and by a steady and constitutional spirit of insolence and cruelty, procured for himself an universal hatred. It is *now* the interest of America to provide for herself. She hath already a large and young family, whom it is more her duty to take care of, than to be granting away her property, to support a power which is become a reproach to the names of men and christians— YE, whose office is to watch over the morals of a nation, of whatsoever sect or denomination ye are of, as well as ye, who are more immediately the guardians of the public liberty, if ye wish to preserve your native country uncontaminated by European corruption, ye must in secret wish a separation. But leaving the moral part to private reflection, I shall chiefly confine my further remarks to the following heads:

First. That it is in the interest of America to be separated from Britain.

Secondly. Which is the easiest and most practicable plan, RECONCILIATION or INDEPENDENCE? with some occasional remarks.

In support of the first, I could if I judged it proper, produce the opinion of some of the ablest and most experienced men on this continent; and whose sentiments on that head are not yet publicly known. It is in reality a self-evident position: foreign dependence, limited in its commerce and cramped and fettered in its legislative powers, can ever arrive at any material eminence. America doth not yet know what opulence is; and although the progress which she hath made stands unparalleled in the history of other nations, it is but childhood, compared with what she should be capable of arriving at, had she, as she ought to have, the legislative powers in her own hands. England is at this time proudly coveting what would do her no good were she to accomplish it; and the continent hesitating on a matter which will be her final ruin if neglected. It is the commerce and not the conquest of America by which England is to be benefitted, and that would in a great measure continue, were the countries as independent of each other as France and Spain; because in many articles neither can go to a better market. But it is the independence of this country of Britain, or any other, which is now the main and only object worthy of contention, and which, like all other truths discovered by necessity, will appear clearer and stronger every day.

First. Because it will come to that one time or other.

Secondly. Because the longer it is delayed, the harder it will be to accomplish.

I have frequently amused myself both in public and private companies, with silently remarking the spacious errors of those who speak without reflecting. And among the many which I have heard, the following seems the most general, viz. that if this rupture should happen forty or fifty years hence, instead of *now*, the Continent would be more able to shake off the dependence. To which I reply, that our military ability, *at this time*, arises from the experience gained in the last war, and which in forty or fifty years time would be totally extinct. The Continent would not, by that time, have a General, or even a military officer left; and we, or those who may succeed us, would be as ignorant of martial matters as the ancient Indians: and this single position, closely attended to, will unanswerably prove that the present time is preferable to all others. The argument turns thus— at the conclusion of the last war, we had experience, but wanted numbers; and forty or fifty years hence, we shall have numbers, without experience; wherefore, the proper point of time, must be some particular point between the two extremes, in which a sufficiency of the former remains, and a proper increase of the latter is obtained: And that point of time is the present time.

The reader will pardon this digression, as it does not properly come under the head I first set out with, and to which I again return by the following position, viz.

Should affairs be patched up with Britain, and she remain the governing and sovereign power of America, (which, as matters are now circumstanced, is giving up the point entirely) we shall deprive ourselves of the very means of sinking the debt we have, or may contract. The value of the back lands, which some of the provinces are clandestinely deprived of by the unjust extension of the limits of Canada, valued only at five pounds sterling per hundred acres, amount to upwards of twenty-five millions Pennsylvania currency; and the quit-rents at one penny sterling per acre, to two millions yearly.

It is by the sale of those lands that the debt may be sunk without burden to any, and the quit-rent reserved thereon, will always lessen, and in time will wholly support the yearly expense of government. It matters not how long the debt is in paying, so that the lands when sold be applied to the discharge of it, and for the execution of which the Congress, for the time being, will be the continental trustees.

I proceed now to the second head, viz. Which is the easiest and most practicable plan, RECONCILIATION or INDEPENDENCE? with some occasional remarks.

He who takes nature for his guide, is not easily beaten out of his argument, and on that ground,

I answer *generally*—*That* INDEPENDENCE *being a* SINGLE SIMPLE LINE, *contained within ourselves; and reconciliation, a matter exceedingly perplexed and complicated, and in which a treacherous, capricious court is to interfere, gives the answer without a doubt.*

The present state of America is truly alarming to every man who is capable of reflection. Without law, without government, without any other mode of power than what is founded on, and granted by, courtesy. Held together by an unexampled concurrence of sentiment, which is nevertheless subject to change, and which every secret enemy is endeavoring to dissolve. Our present condition is Legislation without law; wisdom without a plan; a Constitution without a name; and, what is strangely astonishing, perfect independence contending for dependence. The instance is without a precedent; the case never existed before; and who can tell what may be the event? The property of no man is secure in the present unbraced system of things. The mind of the multitude is left at random, and seeing no fixed object before them, they pursue such as fancy or opinion presents. Nothing is criminal; there is no such thing as treason; wherefore, every one thinks himself at liberty to act as he pleases. The tories dared not have assembled offensively, had they known that their lives, by that act, were forfeited to the laws of the state. A line of distinction should be drawn between English soldiers taken in battle, and inhabitants of America taken in arms. The first are prisoners, but the latter traitors. The one forfeits his liberty, the other his head.

Notwithstanding our wisdom, there is a visible feebleness in some of our proceedings which gives encouragement to dissensions. The Continental belt is too loosely buckled. And if something is not done in time, it will be too late to do anything, and we shall fall into a state in which neither *reconciliation* nor *independence* will be practicable. The King and his worthless adherents are got at their old game of dividing the Continent, and there are not wanting among us Printers who will be busy in spreading specious falsehoods. The artful and hypocritical letter which appeared a few months ago in two of the New-York papers, and likewise in others, is an evidence that there are men who want either judgment or honesty.

It is easy getting into holes and corners and talking of reconciliation: But do such men seriously consider how difficult the task is, and how dangerous it may prove, should the Continent divide thereon? Do they take within their view all the various orders of men whose situation and circumstances, as well as their own, are to be considered therein. Do they put themselves in the place of the sufferer whose *all* is *already* gone, and of the soldier, who hath quitted *all* for the defence of his country? If their ill-judged moderation be suited to their own private situations *only*, regardless of others, the event will convince them that "they are reckoning without their Host."

Put us, say some, on the footing we were in the year 1763: To which I answer, the request is not *now* in the power of Britain to comply with, neither will she propose it; but if it were, and even should it be granted, I ask, as a reasonable question, by what means is such a corrupt and faithless court to be kept to its engagements? Another parliament, nay, even the present, may hereafter repeal the obligation, on the pretense of its being violently obtained, or unwisely granted; and in that case, where is our redress?—No going to law with nations; cannon are the barristers of crowns; and the sword, not of justice, but of war, decides the suit. To be on the footing of 1763, it is not sufficient that the laws only be put in the same state, but that our circumstances, likewise, be put in the same state; Our burnt and destroyed towns repaired, or built up, our private losses made good, our public debts (contracted for defence) discharged; otherwise, we shall be millions worse than we were at that enviable period. Such a request, had it been complied with a year ago, would have won the heart and the soul of the Continent—but now it is too late, "the Rubicon is passed."

Besides, the taking up arms, merely to enforce the repeal of a pecuniary law, seems as unwarrantable by the divine law, and as repugnant to human feelings, as the taking up arms to enforce obedience thereto. The object, on either side, doth not justify the means; for the lives of men are too valuable to be cast away on such trifles. It is the violence which is done and threatened to our persons; the destruction of our property by an armed force; the invasion of our country by fire and sword, which conscientiously qualifies the use of arms: and the instant in which such a mode of defence became necessary, all subjection to Britain ought to have ceased; and the independence of America should have been considered as dating its era from, and published by, *the first musket that was fired against her.* This line is a line of consistency; neither drawn by caprice, nor extended by ambition; but produced by a chain of events of which the colonies were not the authors.

I shall conclude these remarks with the following timely and well-intended hints. We ought to reflect, that there are three different ways by which an independency may hereafter be effected; and that *one* of those *three* will, one day or other, be the fate of America, viz. By the legal voice of the people in congress; by a military power; or by a mob. It may not always happen that our soldiers are citizens, and the multitude a body of reasonable men; virtue, as I have already remarked, is not hereditary, neither is it perpetual. Should an independency be brought about by the first of those means, we have every opportunity and every encouragement before us, to form the noblest, purest constitution on the face of the earth. We have it in our power to begin the world over again. A situation, similar to the present, hath not happened since the days of Noah until now. The birth-day of a new world is at hand, and a race of men, perhaps as numerous as all Europe contains, are to receive their portion of freedom from the events of a few months. The Reflection is awful—and in this point of view, how trifling, how ridiculous, do the little paltry cavilings of a few weak or interested men appear, when weighed against the business of a world.

Should we neglect the present favorable and inviting period, and independence be hereafter effected by any other means, we must charge the consequence to ourselves, or to those rather, whose narrow and prejudiced souls are habitually opposing the measure, without either inquiring or reflecting. There are reasons to be given in support of independence, which men should rather privately think of, than be publicly told of. We ought not to be debating whether we shall be independent or not, but anxious to accomplish it on a firm, secure and honorable basis, and uneasy rather, that it is not yet begun upon. Every day convinces us of its necessity. Even the tories (if such beings yet remain among us) should, of all men, be the most solicitous to promote it; for as the appointment of committees at first, protected them from popular rage, so a wise and well established form of government will be the only certain means of continuing it securely to them. Wherefore; if they have not virtue enough to be WHIGS, they ought to have prudence enough to wish for independence.

In short, independence is the only BOND that can tie and keep us together. We shall then see our object, and our ears shall be legally shut against the schemes of an intriguing, as well as a cruel enemy. We shall then, too, be on a proper footing to treat with Britain; for there is reason to conclude, that the pride of that court will be less hurt by treating with the American states for terms of peace, than with those whom she denominates "rebellious subjects," for terms of accommodation. It is our delaying it that encourages her to hope for conquest, and our backwardness tends only to prolong the war. As we have, without good effect therefrom, withheld our trade to obtain a redress of our grievances, let us *now* try the alternative, by *independently* redressing them ourselves, and then offering to open the trade. The mercantile and reasonable part of England will be still with us; because peace *with* trade, is preferable to war *without* it. And if this offer be not accepted, other courts may be applied to.

On these grounds I rest the matter. And as no offer hath yet been made to refute the doctrine contained in the former editions of this pamphlet, it is a negative proof that either the doctrine cannot be refuted, or that the party in favor of it are too numerous to be opposed. WHEREFORE, instead of gazing at each other, with suspicious or doubtful curiosity, let each of us hold out to his neighbour the hearty hand of friendship, and unite in drawing a line, which, like an act of oblivion, shall bury in forgetfulness every former dissension. Let the names of Whig and Tory be extinct; and let none other be heard among us, than those of a *good citizen, an open and resolute friend,* and *a virtuous supporter of the* RIGHTS *of* MANKIND, *and of the* FREE AND INDEPENDENT STATES OF AMERICA.